D0184741

PRETTY
POWERFUL
APPEARANCE, SUBSTANCE, AND SUCCESS

PRETTY
POWERFUL
APPEARANCE, SUBSTANCE, AND SUCCESS

EBONI K. WILLIAMS

VIVA
EDITIONS

Published in the United States by Viva Editions, an imprint of Start Midnight, LLC, 101 Hudson Street, Thirty-Seventh Floor, Suite 3705, Jersey City, NJ 07302.

Printed in the United States.
Cover design: Scott Idleman/Blink
Cover photo: Fadil Berisha
Text design: Frank Wiedemann

First Edition.
10 9 8 7 6 5 4 3 2 1

Trade paper ISBN: 978-1-63596-662-6
E-book ISBN: 978-1-63596-663-3

Library of Congress Cataloging-in-Publication Data is available on file.

For my beloved mother, Gloria, who believed in me long before I had the courage to believe in myself.

For my dearly departed aunts, Sherry and Barbara, who through incredible challenges always remained equal parts pretty and powerful.

For our little family's matriarch, Grandmother Katie, you are my heart.

TABLE OF CONTENTS

ACKNOWLEDGEMENTS

Expressing gratitude is something I do every morning when I write a single line in my little personal journal about what I'm most grateful for. I picked up this habit from an episode of *Oprah*. My daily practice of written gratitude is consistent at this point, but I'll admit, I'm shamefully bad at conveying just how deep my gratitude runs to the people who most deserve to know. Here is my feeble attempt to remedy that deficit.

Mother, I could write an entire book expressing all of the lessons you've taught me, and all of the reasons I'm eternally grateful for them and for you. Actually, I intend to do just that one day soon. In the meantime, you should know the gift I'm most grateful for is my faith. Without imposing your faith on to me, you fostered an environment that allowed me to discover God's grace and understanding for myself. You led by example and demonstrated that while the road was not promised to be easy, it was always worth it. Most importantly, you constantly show me that all blessings flow from and through Him, that while I make efforts to follow His will, ultimately I am just a vessel for his work. That's why every day before I go on air, I pray the prayer we prayed together before my very first on-air appearance (as I sat in my car at 3 am nervous out of my mind for my debut on The NFL Network), "God take my tongue and guide it as you would have it deliver the words of your will. In Jesus name, Amen." As I continue on this incredible journey, I know that I can never do anything on my own, it's all Him. He is ordering my steps (remember when you made me sing that song in church as a kid? I wonder if the congregation has forgiven me for assaulting their eardrums?), every single step of the way. My ability to weather the ups and downs of this crazy business is completely due to your fierce installation of an unshakable faith, and my knowing whose I am. I love you forever, Mom.

Christina A. Jackson, when I say this book would not have been possible without you, you know I mean that in the most literal sense. While we settled on the title "Developmental Editor" there is really no title in the world that would adequately describe what you've done for this book. When *Pretty Powerful* was in a state of crisis and on the verge of becoming something that I was not proud of, you stepped in. You took my words and vision and magically wove them together in a way that created a voice and compelling narrative that perfectly fits my idea of what *Pretty Powerful* was always supposed to be. You saved this book and I'll always be grateful to you for that, and for being my rock and best friend for almost 20 years.

All the talent, intelligence, and hard work in the world doesn't matter unless it's coupled with opportunity. I would never have been able to embark on this incredible journey without so many supporters, mentors, and professional thought partners gifting me with unimaginable, life-changing opportunities:

Mo'Kelly, thank you for being the very first person to allow me to dabble in the space of talk radio and flex my legal chops on your program. I didn't even know I wanted to do radio, but your invitation led to the most pivotal moment in my media career.

Robin Bertulucci, thank you for giving a rookie the chance to guest host on the #1 talk radio station in LA. You told me there was a special place in hell for women who didn't help other women, which clearly means there is a special place in heaven for you.

Marc Watts, thank you for mentoring me through this crazy broadcasting business. From the days that I was begging to get on air (thanks for finally letting me take a swing at it on NFL AM) to every consequential television job I've had since, you've been in my corner. I'm eternally grateful.

Bill O'Reilly, no one has ever had a larger platform in cable news, and I'm so very thankful that you chose to share a small part of it with me. Granting me an opportunity to show the world my ability to analyze the law, politics, and culture on your program every week completely changed my career trajectory. Thank you for that.

Sean Hannity, when I was still very green in this business you made the effort to cultivate my talent and encourage me to fight for a multiplatform presence in an industry that prefers to keep talent in narrow boxes. I'll never forget your support and constant positivity. Thank you.

Adrienne Lopez, to the first woman to actually pay me to be on television: thank you, thank you, thank you! A lot of people talk about "value" but you encouraged HLN to actually step up and show that value. I'll always be grateful for that.

Henry Mauldin, when I was still very much trying to figure out the next step, you were a safe and supportive space for me to vent, inquire, and explore. Thank you for experience and wisdom.

Crystal Johns, when I wanted to go from cable free-lancer to CBS News correspondent, you didn't laugh me out of your office. You took me seriously and supported my pairing with the Tiffany Network. That was a real game changer. Thank you.

Matt Sorger and Will Horowitz, being agents for a lawyer is not for the faint-hearted. You two are real pros and you always see the big picture. Your genuine belief in me and my enormous vision is invaluable. I so appreciate you guys.

Craig Schwab, thank you for calling me back! Who says the cold call doesn't work? When I started to miss talk radio you supported my journey back to the micro-phone and together we made WABC history, my friend. Many in this business talk about the need for change and something "different." Very few take that risk, and you did. I'm forever grateful.

Ian Kleinert and Jarred Weisfeld, thank you both for believing in this book. This process has been intense and this book is very special to me. I'm thrilled we were able to work together and share this very personal and powerful book with the world.

Adam Weiss, thank you and the AMWPR Team for

"getting it," and for always being ready to take my professional vision to the next level.

Marcia Clark, Desirée Rogers, Meghan McCain, Judge Jeanine Pirro, Monica Crowley, Kirsten Haglund, and Frank Luntz, you taking time to share your stories, insight, and experience made this book. I am so grateful to each of you.

Before I pursued a career in media, I cut my professional teeth as a legal eagle. Bill Diehl, Kevin Tully, James D. (Butch) Williams, thank you for mentoring me as a young attorney and helping me discover my passion for advocacy and being a voice for the voiceless.

Nothing contributed to shaping my natural intellectual curiosity more than my incredible teachers and professors. Thank you to these brave and selfless educators for lighting a spark in me: Beverly Eury, Jackie Fishman, Jane Prater, Rick Miskolitz, Tom Booker, Jeff Joyce, Jerry Lowe, Dr. Jerma Jackson, Dr. Perry Hall, Dr. Soyini Madison, Shenequa Grey, Esq., and Dr. Winston Riddick.

Finally, this can be a lonely road, so thank you to the women who support, encourage and inspire me with their friendship: Nichelle Sublett, Porscha Elzy, Tory White, KaDarra Lowe, Lauren Lyster, Isabella Rivera, Adrienne Reed, Natalie Robinson, Candice Petty, and Terri Broussard Williams.

EVERY WOMAN

This book is a tribute to every woman. It is for women who know they are exceptional, who desire to be successful, and who strive toward greatness in all the opportunities life presents to them. This book is for those who understand that womanhood is a strength that, when fully embraced, is unstoppable. This book is for and about the *pretty powerful.*

Over time, I have learned there are many tools needed to create the narrative around who I am and what I can offer the world. Learning early and knowing the critical importance of ensuring my substantive competency, I often struggled to reconcile that aspect of myself with the part of me that is, also, very concerned with appearance. After years of working as a commercial actress and model, and competing in pageants, I absolutely put a lot of time and energy into my look, and how I present myself. For many years I felt like a walking-talking contradiction. I also was absolutely serious about what I had to say concerning the law, politics, and social justice (among other things), yet I remained very thoughtful about how I presented physically, how I sounded when I spoke, and what my mannerisms portrayed. I long believed I needed to choose between what was important to me: what I knew (and could do), or what I looked like.

The choice between substance and appearance is a false choice. I was incredibly relieved when I discovered in my own professional journey that with the coexistence of attention to both substance and appearance I feel empowered. I learned that I am able to control the message and professional narrative I want to exude. I can thoughtfully employ my substance and aesthetic to convey exactly what I want to about who I am and what I intend to accomplish.

Pretty powerful is the understanding that as women we have the duality of both "pretty" and "substance" that can (and should) be maximized to achieve any success we set our minds to. Our "pretty" is not a one-size-fits-all prescription, but more accurately, an awareness and leveraging of how we package and present our femininity as an aesthetic that is uniquely authentic and impactful. Our "pretty" is our brand, the visual narrative we create for ourselves, the messaging that screams loudly to all who encounter it. "Substance" (a little easier to grasp and sometimes more comfortable to rely upon) is what we all know it to be. It comes in the form of being ready, prepared, and confident.

This book, for me, has been a labor of love. In it I share personal stories of my family history, childhood experiences that have undoubtedly influenced my thinking, as well as insight into "womanness" from a range of perspectives. It provides a glimpse into the media world through my eyes, commentary from high-powered women who have accomplished magnitudes in the business world, and an advisory for how to navigate potential pitfalls that sometimes present themselves as a result of being a woman with professional ambition. Writing *Pretty Powerful* afforded me the incredible opportunity to speak with dynamic women in law, politics, media, and business who have been through the trenches, paved the way, and inspired me and so many others along the way. Each of them has a personal narrative that reinforced that I am not alone in my very real (and often challenging) experience with the duality of substance and appearance. By sharing their experiences in the White House, prosecuting the highest profile murder case in American history, presiding on the bench, or building a million dollar empire, these women assist me in exploring how we can navigate our professional trajectories while also respecting the importance of our aesthetic. While there are significant challenges along the way that can lead to career stagnation, pettiness from other women, or even sexual harassment, we have incredible choice around how we utilize our appearance, coupled with our substance. When we really understand that choice, we will ultimately achieve whatever successes we set ourselves to achieve.

To the pretty powerful.
Eboni K. Williams, Esq.

"PRETTY" ISN'T A DIRTY WORD

My friends have started having babies faster than I can count. I was speaking with one of my girlfriends from college, and she told me a story about her three year old daughter. She and her daughter were waiting in line at the grocery store when a woman behind them leaned down to my friend's daughter and said "OMG, you're so pretty!" My friend snapped back, "Please don't tell her that! She is also very smart. We don't want her growing up being concerned with the wrong thing."

Now, I can completely understand my friend's preoccupation with making sure her daughter fully appreciates the importance of being an intelligent, bright, and hard-working young woman. But to label "pretty" (i.e. embracing and acknowledging the realistic value assigned to it by the world) as the "wrong" thing to be concerned with, stigmatizes appearance in a way that discounts a very powerful tool in an otherwise fully stocked arsenal; the kind of tool that can take you from good to great, from better to best, and from doing well to winning.

I still remember so clearly the mix of confidence and anticipation I felt on that 16th of July, just over a year ago. I had finally secured what would turn out to be *the* meeting with Fox News executives, which ultimately led to being hired as an on-air legal and political analyst (a coveted position for which I'd been on a long, winding-path pursuit!). I was coming out of a correspondent contract with CBS News, and while I learned a tremendous amount during my stint there (for which I'm very grateful), I was anxious to get on air in time for the 2016 presidential election which was quickly approaching. Not only was I ready to be back on air, but I specifically wanted the air time with the Fox News team. I knew my analysis and dialogue brought a newness, and would be a great fit with the existing team. And more importantly, I had started to grow a real connection to the Fox News viewership. The stakes felt incredibly high.

On-air contributorships are hard to come by. Theoretically, I could have pursued other news outlets, but there was something very compelling about being able to deliver a particularly unique perspective on a network that provides 24/7 news coverage to an unparalleled number of viewers each day. I had met with Fox News executives twice over the past three years, so had some idea what I'd be asked and how the conversation would flow but I didn't want to leave anything to chance. I went into complete preparation mode.

I knew I had to be clear and concise with what I wanted to convey. To say these executives were busy with no time to waste would be an under exaggeration. I would be lucky if the meeting lasted longer than fifteen or twenty minutes.

I knew I'd have to maximize each moment I had their attention in that room, and do my best to make an impact. My mission was to persuade these hiring executives that I would be a value-add to this company. It was a tall order because Fox News is the reigning cable news network by many miles. So why did they need me? That was the question I was responsible for answering in that meeting, and if I didn't answer it to their satisfaction, my dreams of covering this election on Fox News would be over. I needed to convey that I was knowledgeable, credible, and professional. But they had a million people on staff who already fit that description. I needed to offer something different: a fresh, unique, relatable presence that pushed the boundaries of what the network's viewers expected.

I consciously thought through each element and came up with specific ways to get the point across for each one. In addition to what I planned to verbalize to these executives, I knew that my mere presence and presentation would send a message long before I uttered a word. I knew I'd be assessed by what I looked like when I walked into that room. In addition to all my preparation for the conversation, I also thought seriously about what I would wear, how I would style my hair, and what my makeup would look like.

Now, before you write those concerns off as superficial, consider the reality that the very first impression most of us make is based on physical appearance. When we encounter someone, before we engage in conversation, we all make assessments about what that person values and what they can offer based on what you think about their physical appearance. It can be a taboo reality, but a reality nonetheless. Ultimately, I decided on a bright vermilion sheath dress with a high neckline and hem that hit right at the knees (a well-covered, but still feminine dress silhouette), nude stiletto pumps (a conservatively colored "daytime" shoe), minimal bronzy makeup, and loose waves in my hair (to add a little ease to the ensemble). That look, to me, sent the message that I am a serious professional, with a classic personality and respect for family values, but with a fresh, youthful energy.

We proceeded to have a twenty minute conversation where I recalled my courtroom experience, my time in post-Katrina Louisiana politics, and training at various other media outlets. After I sold my ability to be fair and reasonable but firm with a point of view, completely prepared for commentary on a wide range of topics, and strong enough to go toe to toe with Bill O'Reilly each week, I was told by an executive that I seemed like a "tough cookie" and was offered the job.

Fox News was launched in 1996 by Roger Ailes, a man whose professional background was a hybrid of politics and entertainment as he advised presidents Nixon, Reagan, and George H. W. Bush, but started his career as a producer for the "Mike Douglas Show." Ailes passed away in 2017, but read any book about him and you'll learn that when he launched Fox News he had an unwavering understanding that television is a visual medium. During a meeting I had with Ailes shortly after joining the network as a contributor, he told me, "What it looks like matters. What you say and how you say it matters, too. But every news executive in the country has at least four broadcasts on at any one time. They are trying to anticipate what audiences want. Audiences will go with great news, but first it needs to catch their eye." Ailes then asked me to look at the screens and tell him where my eye went. I told him, "I'm drawn to Governor Nikki Haley." Haley was wearing a yellow jacket in an interview that she was doing on a competing network. Ailes was not pleased about the competing network part, but he made his point. My eye went to what was visually appealing and then I wanted to hear what she had to say. Whether I stayed tuned was up to what she said and how she said it.

As such, what you look like matters, a lot. When you provide news coverage, some people see being concerned with the visual appeal as a contradiction to your substantive work. Not Ailes. He understood that this attention to the visual appeal was what made television news, and particularly cable news where you are charged with holding an audience's attention at all times, which is different from print or radio. In a multimedia society people can consume their news from anywhere, including social media now. The burden is on these networks to provide the best overall product, and Ailes made no secret of his ambition to deliver news content that also looked better than anything else available. Fox News has been the number one rated cable news network for fifteen of the twenty years it's been on air.

I can never know the exact determining factor in being extended that offer, but I am certain that if I didn't "look the part," I would not have even had the opportunity to have that conversation about my other, more merit-based qualifications. Studies have shown that good looks help you get ahead in business, whether you're a woman *or* a man. Specifically, it's shown that aesthetically pleasing people are usually hired sooner, get promotions more quickly, and are paid more than their less-aesthetically pleasing coworkers. In fact, if you're a man, attributes like a full head of hair, wearing tailored suits, and being tall all make you more likely to be paid attention to and convey authority and to have others (men and women) want to be around you. Those traits absolutely make a man's aesthetic a part of his power ascent. It's been speculated that good looks helped the political ascents of many men including President John F. Kennedy, former Democratic vice-presidential nominee John Edwards and Canadian Prime Minister Justin Trudeau. But it's also clear that while these factors can impact a man's professional journey, that impact is nowhere near as prevalent as how much a woman's appearance affects her power ascent.

I'm not suggesting that this immediate aesthetic evaluation is right or wrong. I am asserting that it is real and persistent. While your look matters more when you work in certain industries like television or entertainment, how you physically present matters in business, the law, real estate, and almost every other profession. No matter what industry you're in, every industry is about branding and messaging, and how you look plays a large part in that.

I was taught this lesson long before entering the news industry. I learned it as a child. I had my first headshots taken at six years old when I was signed to a local talent agency in Charlotte, North Carolina where I grew up. Much of my mother's parenting style was adopted by her observing the trajectories of highly successful people. My mother watched successful women around her and noticed that there were quite a few dynamics at play. She figured out that for me to have the best chance for success, I needed to employ as many of those attributes as possible. She knew that teaching me how to tap into my femininity, personality, and attractiveness would only bolster my power source and unlock an even broader scope of opportunity. After repeatedly being told that I would be good for commercials, my mother tried to make good on what seemed like public opinion and took me to an agency's open casting call. I was signed on the spot. I quickly started getting called into auditions for various commercials. Everything from grocery stores, car companies, and clothing retailers would hold castings where I and all the other hopefuls would go and present in-person. The company representatives would take a look at us, possibly ask us to say a few words, and decide if we were a good fit for their brand. Would we be able to persuade the public to buy the company's product?

In addition to commercial gigs, I was also competing in pageants as a young child. One day after a ballet class my mother sacrificed to put me in (after taking her cue from the affluent parents whose children she drove on a school bus as one of her part-time jobs), a classmate's grandmother asked my mother if she had ever considered entering me into a beauty pageant. Pageants were a rich girl sport, and since we could barely afford the activities I was already participating in, the answer was "no." This woman insisted that pageants were another way to broaden my horizons and enhance my confidence, sportsmanship, and the all-important "stage presence" (all amazing tools for success). She assured my mother that the expensive entry fees and wardrobe costs could be covered by sponsors, and that I could even win college scholarships if I performed well. The words "college scholarship" were music to my mother's ears, and within a month I was competing in my first pageant.

My first competition was a preliminary contest, otherwise known as a "local" pageant, which ultimately led to the state finals for the title "Miss Cinderella," an international scholarship pageant that for thirty years has been the largest and most prestigious scholarship-oriented pageant of its kind. These experiences were my introduction to understanding that the way I looked was a value-add.

After many years of auditioning for, booking, and shooting commercials, and participating in over fifteen pageant competitions—sometimes winning, sometimes left standing in the background (painfully) clapping as first runner up—I figured out something very important: if I could successfully yield my look to sell a product and market myself as an organization (or a state, even!), I could also yield my look to sell a message. Everything about your appearance is an opportunity to convey something intentionally important. This notion drives the concept of being *Pretty Powerful*, and my realization around it serves as motivation to share these stories in this book.

While my mother was unapologetically aware that what we learned was a commercially appealing look, she was never naive to the short-term nature of aesthetic value. Coming from generational poverty, my mother also knew to instill the lessons of academic success, education, and professional ambition from the time I was in kindergarten. She had a simple saying, "poor people don't have time to play." She made it known that while the pageants and commercials I participated in on the weekends were extracurricular and part of my development, nothing would better position me to escape our economic situation than a full education.

My mother remains a woman with enormous expectations. From the time I started school, she demanded academic excellence. B's were unacceptable. When I would question why it was necessary to make all A's all the time or end up on the receiving end of severe discipline, her answer was that I could not afford to be average in any way. She made it clear that as a young black girl from a poor neighborhood, there were lots of preconceived notions about who I was and what I could offer the world. To curb those negative narratives, I would have to employ every tool and develop a fully stocked arsenal to demonstrate excellence.

Her message was clear: being a pretty girl could get me into the room, so that was important, but it would never keep me there. If I intended to stay in any room long enough to make a real change and ascend to any position of power, I would need to possess substantive excellence and impeccable credibility. That is why grades counted, degrees mattered, and work ethic and experience were important. That is also a large part of why going to law school and becoming a member of the American Bar Association became my dream.

Now, being a credentialed practitioner of the law affords me many gifts, but the most valuable one is credibility. I know I'm ready for the competition. When I walk into any room with my aesthetic carefully considered and my credentials known, I am unstoppable, and any woman who leverages the balance between her optimal aesthetic and her hard-earned substance will be the same.

CHAPTER 1

A Cautionary Tale

From an early age I learned the immeasurably valuable lesson that everything about your appearance is an opportunity to convey something about yourself. I continue to practice this same thoughtfulness—which served me throughout my college entrance interviews, law firm interviews, and court appearances as a practicing attorney—everyday as a Fox News contributor where my goal is to deliver legal and political analysis in a way that resonates its truth and power with the viewers who consume it.

In deciding to wear my hair up to an appearance, I am deliberately saying I want to be taken more seriously and deflect my sex appeal. A choice to wear white may be an effort to balance a particularly difficult argument I need to make about rape or gun violence. If I want to have the ability to make a very aggressive argument about a client or issue, a neckline that shows more skin is a good decision, but never so much cleavage as to undermine my credibility and ability. So much about the thought process of presentation is about cultivating an intention on the front end and then making choices about appearance based on that intention. There are times for a woman in business that may call for a relaxed tone and temperament to achieve a goal, consequently the look might need to depart from a strictly traditional or conservative business look. Likewise, if a meeting calls for a more assertive or demanding transaction, it is wise to balance that with a softer, more feminine look. This is a bold strategy for women to seize the opportunity to define, own, and achieve a successful professional agenda, but as we know, success isn't defined by "prettiness" alone. Short-changing the substantive part of the equation when tapping into pretty power—which can be tempting because it requires time-consuming hard work to earn—will inevitably result in failure.

As I write this book, a chief concern of promoting "pretty" as powerful has the potential to be misleading. Questions circle around the possibility that readers could misinterpret the title as implying that simply being pretty is enough to leverage power. To be clear, it is not. In fact, the proportions of substance and style are (in most cases) not even equal. An interpretation of the *Pretty Powerful* premise to mean style over substance as the pathway to power and success is missing the point. And any woman who elects to focus on looks, at the exclusion of developing substantive building blocks, will do themselves a tremendous disservice.

The significance of that imbalance cannot be overstated. The time and effort spent on maximizing the aesthetic can become a complete waste if the investment to be substantively capable is not already in place. It is a mistake only to place value on great hair, makeup, and wardrobe. Resources must be committed to attaining academic credentials, relevant professional experience, and the highly important strong work ethic to have the best chance at achieving your goals.

Conversely, however, it is also a mistake in many situations to rely on substance alone. The balance of the duality is necessary, but delicate, as you'll hear reiterated in countless considerations throughout the book. In the wake of a widely discussed (and arguably the most attention-getting) election cycle, it seems fitting to begin with examples of a few of America's most-recognized female politicians.

Governor Sarah Palin successfully captured the world's attention with her charm, perceived femininity, and aesthetic appeal when she was first selected to be the Republican party's nominee for the vice-presidency in 2008. But quickly her substantive vulnerability began to show, and she was unable to convert that initial currency into points on the board.

Even though most Americans' first real introduction to Palin was over ten years ago, she's still a great example to analyze. For a lot of us Millennial-ish, on the cusp women, she was one of the first women who we saw running for a vice-presidency. We missed Geraldine Ferraro, so Palin was it for us, and was one of the first women to be a mother and do it with cross-aisle appeal. For a lot of us, there was something very exciting about it, so to see her, narratively speaking, crumble in a way that started to cast her as not having the goods to back up the sense of possibility was huge.

Republican presidential nominee John McCain found himself running for the highest office in the world against a young, dynamic political phenomenon named Barack Obama. The seventy-two-year-old Republican needed help, and he seemed to have found it in Palin. She was the sitting governor from Alaska and she was exactly what the flailing McCain campaign needed. The first-term governor was in many ways the remedy the GOP needed for their Obama problem. At forty-two years old she was the youngest governor in Alaska's history as well as the state's first female chief state officer. She had a successful record as a local mayor before becoming governor, but Alaska is not exactly the presidential swing state that Ohio or Florida is, so why did the McCain campaign select this unknown governor? She had pretty power in spades. One look at Palin and her classic physical beauty is apparent. With her slim, yet feminine frame, bright white megawatt smile, and big brown eyes, it's no wonder that she placed second runner up at the Miss Alaska pageant. In addition to her aesthetic appeal, she also mastered a charming, folksy, feminine, yet powerful appeal that came across in her speech cadence and physicality. Her smile, winks, and general warmth all read as inviting and attractive.

Even Palin's tough talking, red-meat ideology was welcomed by many in her base. Perhaps because the inflammatory rhetoric was wrapped in her high-pitched vocal inflection, it was particularly palatable and enjoyable. From pure looks, to delivery, to charm, Palin was hitting all the right notes. But then came the questions.

"Sarah Palin was someone in a moment in time with enormous potential and enormous talent. The tragedy of Sarah Palin is her not being able to grow beyond her limitations," is how senior advisor to the McCain

Campaign, Steve Schmidt put it. When interviewed in the PBS documentary series "16 for '16 – The Contenders," Schmidt also stated, "We just didn't know until about three days after we picked her, how manifestly unqualified she was."

There is no doubt that Palin's "pretty" (her womanhood and her relatable, standardly attractive physical appearance) existed as an unignorable aspect of her total value as a public figure. In the end, though, there turned out to be insurmountable evidence that raised questions about her substantive qualifications.

On September 11, 2008, Palin sat down with ABC News's Charlie Gibson. Gibson was on the short list to publicly vet the young governor's qualifications for being a seventy-two-year-old's heartbeat away from the most powerful position in the world. After the interview, it was painfully obvious that Palin had absolutely no idea what the Bush Doctrine was. Even when Gibson gave her the answer on a silver platter, she still was unable to synthesize it into thoughtful, applicable analysis around her position concerning this basic foreign policy.

The Gibson interview was bad, but Palin is probably most infamous for her series of interviews with Katie Couric. During this series, there were a plethora of incoherent answers around everything from national security to economic policy and American history. Most notable though was Palin's inability to name even one specific newspaper that she read prior to being added to the Republican presidential ticket.

Particularly concerning is that Couric framed the question around Palin's reading of such papers as a way of informing her worldview. Having an informed worldview is a necessary trait for people we befriend, date, or do business with. It is a particularly important requirement for someone seeking the second highest office of the land. Palin simply could not or would not do it. In the years since the interview Couric has said that she felt Palin's nonanswer to her newspaper question was more about frustration with Couric for the way she asked the question, than Palin's actual inability to name a newspaper. One could argue that just because she couldn't or wouldn't name a newspaper doesn't mean she lacks a worldview, but her nonanswer certainly does raise suspicions around what that worldview is and how exactly it is informed. Palin also could not name a single U.S. Supreme Court decision she disagreed with. Instead she defaulted to a general argument that she would disagree with any decision that removes power from the local level and hands it to the federal government. Again, not a pure indictment of Palin's intelligence, but another incredibly suspicious nonanswer.

In November 2015, political website *The Hill* asked Palin about her response to Couric's question about her news sources. Palin said, "I had a crappy answer. But it was a fair question. I didn't like, though, the way that, forever then in these seven years, that interview has kind of been stamped on my forehead as, 'she's an idiot.' I just think, in the context of the whole ball of wax that day— or two days—of an interview and editing, it wasn't real fun." Palin's reflection is a material example of the kind of impact that persists when anyone—but especially a woman, and even more so an attractive woman—demonstrates cracks in the veneer.

The media certainly didn't help Palin's case. In addition

to the implosions during high-profile interviews were the severely damaging *Saturday Night Live* skits. Tina Fey's portrayal of Palin was so convincing that there were a series of studies that became known as the "Fey Effect." The studies found that people so believed that Fey's portrayal emulated exact words from Palin, that young republicans and independents (because democrats showed no change after viewing the clips) were less likely to vote for the McCain ticket. Essentially the SNL skits were as, if not more, damaging than various attacks from political opponents.

As most studies show, being attractive is a professional advantage to a point, but that advantage can contort into a handicap for women because the assumption is that attractive young women don't know anything. This ignorant assumption has been called the "Bimbo Effect." Palin was absolutely subject to those assumptions. Despite her self-inflicted wounds on the campaign trail, Palin was also a victim of the media's (and society's) sexism. A clear example of this was a photograph that was widely circulated of a young man looking up on stage from the crowd. Sounds harmless enough, except that the photo was framed from between Palin's legs, making the boy appear to be looking up her skirt. In response to the photo's wide circulation Palin responded, "It's a telltale sign of a little bit of sexism in our society." She's right.

Another woman who learned just how quickly people were to question her lack of knowledge simply because she was an attractive woman, was Geraldine Ferraro. In 1984 Ferraro became the first woman to be named to the ticket of a major party for the presidency, when she was the Democrats' nominee for vice-president. Similar to Palin's announcement twenty-four years later, Ferraro enjoyed an initial honeymoon with the media and the public after her candidacy was announced. Also like Palin, Ferraro was quickly scrutinized about her looks, family life, and intellectual fitness. While Ferraro was a teacher turned successful New York City prosecutor, she was not spared harsh questions around her substantive qualifications to be in the White House. During her debate against George H. W. Bush, Bush proceeded to "help Ms. Ferraro out" by explaining foreign policy to her on stage. Ferraro did not appreciate it and quickly called Bush out on his condescending tone and statement.

Ferraro said that it was never enough to be "as good" as men, that women always needed to be a little bit better than men just to be seen as equal. I believe that to be true. There is simply almost zero margin for error when it comes to women because of the preconceived notions around women relying exclusively on their appearance to bring them success. Therefore, the effectiveness of this dual-threat, style-meets-substance approach, is only viable when there is compelling evidence of said woman's intellectual prowess.

And then there is former Secretary of State Hillary Clinton. Her tale is a different one from those of Palin and Ferraro, but cautionary nonetheless. It is one that reminds us of both sides of being *Pretty Powerful,* and how even the most substantive woman with the most substantive agenda will also be held to the fire for her looks. No woman has endured more political scrutiny and analysis in our country than Clinton. From her time as first lady, serving in the U.S. Senate, as secretary of state, to her two runs at the White House, we have collectively picked this woman apart. Arguably, when you're running to be the leader of the free world, you should be subjected to incredible levels of dissection. What's not arguable is that the level of scrutiny around Clinton is utterly unprecedented when compared to her male counterparts on both sides of the aisle, including President Barack Obama and 2016 Republican presidential nominee Donald Trump.

And her look was not off limits. We've heard Clinton's pantsuits mocked for decades. Her hairstyles have included bobs, bangs, ponytails, short cropped cuts, and shoulder length tresses all in an attempt to look most attractive and appropriate, and the media have commented on every single attempt. Clinton's campaign so clearly understood the pretty power effect on effective messaging that they brought in *Vogue* magazine's editor-in-chief, Anna Wintour, as a style consultant for the 2016 presidential campaign.

There is no time when messaging and controlling the narrative is more important than when you're running for president. That is why Wintour was tasked to avoid outrageously expensive brands and to stick to American designers (a lesson around creating the right packaging for the right audience and role we'll touch on throughout the book). As should have been predicted, Clinton experienced social media backlash when she wore a $12,495 Armani jacket during a speech on income inequality. Meanwhile Trump frequently wears Brioni suits that retail for $5,250 to $6,900. Trump is also a bona fide celebrity in addition to being a presidential candidate, so perhaps he is granted more slack on the issue.

Appearance took center stage at the 2016 Republican and Democratic National Conventions. People were buzzing about Melania Trump's dress almost as much as the controversy about the originality of her speech. The would-be first lady wore a stunning white dress by Roksanda Ilinčić. The dress, which retails for $2,190, was sold out online within mere hours. Also, many felt Melania's decision bucked tradition by donning a Serbian-born designer's ensemble instead of wearing an American designer. (We learned later that the statement was intentional and strategic. Ilinčić's personal narrative is very similar to Melania's. Both women came from similar parts of the world—Melania from Slovenia and Ilinčić from Serbia—and both women found their way out through a career in fashion. Two all-American dreams come true. But criticized even so.)

Wearing white was also a (intentional?) theme of sorts at both conventions. While Melania donned the white dress, Clinton accepted her party's nomination wearing a white pantsuit by Ralph Lauren. Speculation around why each woman wore white is broad. Many were quick to point out Clinton's choice as elegant, sophisticated, and presidential as well as her way to pay homage to the women in the Suffrage movement who often wore white when protesting to create a clear, recognizable political identity while furthering their cause, and evoking a message of purity. Some also suggested Clinton elected to wear white in an effort to reshape narratives around her trustworthiness. At the time of her nomination, she was polling at less than forty percent of Americans seeing her as trustworthy. The white suit could have been an attempt to rebrand her as pure, honest, and even angelic. Similarly, some speculated Melania wore white in an attempt to underscore the purity of her husband's motives and morality in his pursuit of the White House. Obviously, it will take more to wash away the sins of Clinton or Trump than white clothes, but do not underestimate the power of the visual cue.

While some scoffed at the addition of an actual stylist being added to Clinton's political campaign, what you wear and how you wear it is a huge part of messaging and branding, and that is serious business in itself (especially in the serious business of politics). Highlighting this point is the fact that many times stylists are used to minimize, rather than enhance, the role of fashion in a candidate's life. It is absolutely true that clothes, hair, makeup, and jewelry can be distracting (for the lauded and applauded) and get in the way of the message you are really trying to deliver. That is why women, even those of us who operate without a professional stylist, are fully mindful of what not to wear, as well as what to wear to cast ourselves in the best image of our intended narrative. Being mindful is just the first step to being able to convincingly convey it to everyone else.

A woman's style always speaks before she does and we should utilize that power to communicate positive messages and influence perceptions. Even if you're not running for political office in today's social media saturated world, what you look like is an incredibly important messaging tool. Every professional woman is charged with crafting a personal brand, and in doing so should absolutely take seriously what her "pretty" package—clothes, hair, makeup, accessories, and other visual affects—is communicating about her, and then be fully prepared to back it all up.

CHAPTER 2

THE COMFORT ZONE

With insight from Desirée Rogers

"I think I confuse people. In [America], there is a bias against people who have a certain look or style. I have fought this all of my life. People only see this package, and it's a tall and vocal package. So people think, 'Wait a minute, you can't be this stylish and intelligent, too.' I take people out of their comfort zone."

—DESIRÉE ROGERS

It's called "lethal fabulousness."

An epitomic phrase coined by *Huffington Post* blogger Michele Langevine Leiby in a 2010 post with her analysis and perspective of Desirée Glapion Rogers. In her (and many others') expressed opinion, Rogers was pegged as being what many called a "flashy" woman during her (short) stint as White House social secretary for President Obama back in 2009. That "flashiness" presented a crippling challenge to Rogers's perceived success (and like-ability) in the political role. It's a concept that the blogger also personally identified with as a woman whose professional achievements—though impactful and many—were often overshadowed by her look. Her beautifully high-end wardrobe, her perfectly paired accessories, her overall look of "fabulousness" is a concept that I absolutely identify with as a woman who is (has been, and will always be) very intentional about my look. The way I present is a choice that I've made with purpose, but to Rogers's mention, doesn't make people comfortable.

This concept is one of the real potential pitfalls of pretty power, but I assert the best way to overcome it is to know how to navigate and expect, not to be guilty about and try to avoid all together. Rogers has a few things to say about the matter. She was gracious enough to speak with me recently and share some of her thoughts around an issue with which she has such intimate knowledge.

But before we dive into some of the consequences of lethal fabulousness, it's only fair (and makes the lethality of Rogers's fabulousness all the more puzzling) to start by looking at all that makes this woman a credible power player in any sense of the term. Presently, Rogers serves as the chief executive officer of Fashion Fair, a cosmetic line for women of color. She's served as CEO of this division of Johnson Publishing Company (the Chicago-based, African American owned and operated publisher responsible for the iconic magazines *Ebony* and *Jet*) since 2010. In her role, she's been credited with bold organizational changes (for the better), revitalized website marketing, solid ad-page jumps and increased circulation demands for the company's magazines only months into her tenure. She shared that as

CEO of Fashion Fair, her journey as a businesswoman (and all the experiences that come with those endeavors along the way) have absolutely informed her vision for the brand.

When it comes to business, Rogers is a force and understands the enormity of her position. She shared that "Because of my vast experience in business, I was completely humbled to lead this company. Humbled by what the brand represents, and the great mountains that have been moved by incredible women like Mrs. Johnson, who founded the line 45 years ago." In a move of true leadership, she was smart to tap into that humility and take the helm of the company in a way that respected everyone who'd been there before her, instead of immediately jumping in with the assumption that her experience trumped all. I mean, she clearly had proven her ability to land such a role, but she approached it with understanding. She recounted her strategy, sharing, "I also didn't want to be overwhelmed by the rich history, so I did a lot of listening when I first came to the company (and I still do). I listened to the current consumer, our partners around the country, I spent time behind the counter in the U.S. and in Europe in order to gauge the perception of the line."

Rogers easily articulated the three ideals she and her team work hard to convey and represent through the Fashion Fair brand. It's quite easy to see a little bit of each in ourselves and the powerful women around us. There's The Rebel: Like the late creator of Fashion Fair, Eunice W. Johnson. Rogers said, "We want to honor the rebel in all women. The courage and guts that it took to launch a line specifically with women of color in mind, particularly when no one else was doing that was incredible and powerful. It's hard to imagine now, [according to Nielsen, black women spend an estimated $7.5 billion annually on beauty products] but at that time no line of cosmetics truly tried to offer a full color range to complement our varied complexions. From the darkest to lightest shades and the varying pink, red and golden undertones, it was important to Mrs. Johnson that all of that diversity of beauty be represented. We work today to salute the rebel in all women." And there's no doubt (as we'll talk about more later) that Rogers must see (and be reminded of) the rebel in her all too often.

And then there's The Magician. "Makeup is magic. It can make you look like your best self and in the hands of a woman or makeup artist it can create magic. Whether it's a simple swipe of mascara or a more audacious lip color, makeup is magical." Now this is a concept to which I and my fellow makeup lovers can so easily relate. Sure, on a normal day of running errands, or a hectic travel day, you won't catch me with a stitch on, but when I get ready to step onto set, host a panel, or just go out to a nice dinner with friends, you'll see me with my face well-made and carefully "beat" (as they say when a face of makeup is done flawlessly) . . . it truly is magical!

Rogers also spoke about The Wish Granter, reminding us that "Dreams do come true. [Fashion Fair] works to honor and uplift women as they seek to fulfill all of their dreams. This includes supporting the volunteer and mentorship efforts of the people who work for Fashion Fair. Just like the 'glow' of what Mrs. Johnson did by donating over $55 million to charity through the Fashion Fair Fashion Shows. Fashion Fair remains an authentic place women (especially women of color) can come to make their dreams come true."

Since becoming the CEO of Fashion Fair, Rogers's power has been unstoppable. She's been leading in a way that no one can deny. For many, Desirée Rogers's notoriety developed while serving as White House social secretary, but her solid background, exceptional education, and ambitious professional accomplishments far overshadow any superficial critique based on aesthetic . . . or at least they should.

Rogers's path is the perfect mix of substance and style. Born in New Orleans, Louisiana to a civically engaged father, Roy E. Glapion, Jr., city councilman and Zulu Organization king for over a decade, her cultural roots run deep and are very much a part of who she is. She grew up with parents who instilled the importance of manners and expected poise.

After graduating from the all-girls private school, Academy of the Sacred Heart in New Orleans, she matriculated at Wellesley College in Massachusetts—the top women's college in the nation—from which she received a bachelor's degree in political science. Rogers went immediately into Harvard Business School for graduate school and participated in the Women and Power Program. After receiving her MBA, she married John Rogers, Jr., the chairman and CEO of Ariel Investments, a Chicago-based mutual fund firm. The two divorced after twelve years and have a daughter that they amicably co-parent together.

Rogers graduated and hit the ground running when, only a few years after, her leadership career was launched with an appointment by Governor Jim Edgar to assume the position of director of the Illinois Lottery. At the time she was the youngest cabinet member of the $1.5 billion agency. As director, she launched the first Illinois Mega

Millions along with five other states, overhauled instant-ticket games, and grew the business from $300 million to $600 million.

Rogers's next roles were with Peoples Energy as VP for corporate communications, chief marketing officer, and senior VP for customer service. She eventually became president of Peoples Gas and North Shore Gas where she served from 2003–07. Each of her executive leadership roles required confidence, persistence, long-term vision, and drive . . . and she handled each one gracefully. It was undoubtedly her grace and capability that landed her the role as special assistant to the president, social secretary for the White House, in 2009, the first African American to hold the position. But it was also in the role of social secretary that all of her preparation, all of her greatness, all of her fabulousness started being perceived as everything but an asset.

In 2009, Rogers assumed a coveted position on a presidential team. As expected (and should have been anticipated by any prepared individual), she was immediately pulled out of the enterprise world into one of political context. It would be safe to assume that she'd understood the adjustments she'd have to make, and the differences between functioning as a leader in business and in government. What she (and everyone else) was not prepared for, was how much she'd be propelled into the spotlight, and the intense scrutiny that would come with it.

Even before assuming the post, "stylish," "sophisticated," "polished," and "headstrong," were words that publicly described this five-foot-ten beautiful master of branding, marketing, and networking. How could she not be a woman who knew her own greatness? Shouldn't she be proud of the hard work and determination she'd put into her studies at prestigious institutions? Of the long hours and grind she put into each of her leadership-level roles? Of the well-heeled family who supported her along the way? Her presence and confidence could not be ignored. And her stunning looks and almost perfect presentation of luxury branded wardrobe classics, finely chosen accessories and pristine pixie haircut should've added to the brand of a social planner. It may sound superficial (and make us dig deeper to question why), but people like to party with the "good-looking." But in this case, Rogers was consistently singled-out for being *too* fabulous.

In her *Huffington Post* article, writer Leiby asserts that "[Rogers] of the Louboutin stilettos and Comme des Garçons gown never quite fit in in a town where sensible heels and navy blue and charcoal gray business suits are the dress code for most working women." That town, of course, is Washington, DC, The Federal City. Does the essence of that statement still hold true after so many years? Is "traditional" conservative dress required to be taken seriously as a woman, and was Rogers's personal style and indisputable presence (largely influenced by her aesthetic) prohibitive to her success (and acceptance)? Or is there maybe a certain level that would've been accepted, but Rogers was just too fabulous to fall below that (some could argue) arbitrary line?

There is such an expectation when it comes to the way public officials should present, and although Rogers felt she'd made the necessary adjustments to her standard way of presenting to the world—by wearing more button-ups, blazers, pantsuits, and toned-down colors by day—the bigness of her natural presence could not go overlooked. She was consistently invited for interviews, asked to be photographed, appearing at fashion shows with the likes of Anna Wintour, former long-time editor-in-chief at *Vogue*.

Rogers shared that she was "most shocked by the lack of reception I received when I took the role in DC. There was an expectation that I would 'fit in' and I simply didn't." I pushed back and cited examples when Rogers did conform to the more traditional "DC uniform" of dark suits and asked her if she wore that everyday if she thought it would make a difference? She didn't think so. She said, "I don't think it would have made a difference. They simply were not ready for a woman like me in DC in [the social secretary] role. It wasn't because of my education or anything like that. I was proud and happy to serve my friends in the White House and to serve my country. But there was always this undercurrent. I hate to say it, but maybe a bit of racism. This feeling of 'who is this person wearing the same dress that I have?'"

Rogers shared a personal story to support her point. "There was a woman who approached me at an event and told me that she had just purchased the dress I was wearing. I didn't immediately pick up on all of the energy in her comment, so I responded by telling her that it was incredibly comfortable and I was sure she would enjoy it once she wore it. What I later realized is that there was resentment in her voice and a negative intention around her comment. It was a read." Rogers had many moments like that one, reminding her that her aesthetic was very much a point of contention, when all she was doing was getting dressed to go to work every day!

She shared, "The focus was on my clothes, but that

was just a catalyst for the real message they dare not speak. Clothes became a foil to criticize what was really a problem for them; a presumption around my access that made them very uncomfortable."

Rogers was performing well in her role as social engineer extraordinaire, bringing a different taste-level and powerful people to hundreds of unique White House social events like open-mic nights and intimate serenades by iconic musical artists. But much of that job success was being distracted by her unapologetic allure. She accepted interview requests and spoke assertively.

It was not uncommon for Rogers to be introduced on national news segments and the like as the "Eye catching, glamorous, social secretary," not the "Well-prepared, capable social secretary." She was named the best dressed woman in DC by the *Huffington Post*, and appeared on the cover of the *Wall Street Journal* even before former first lady Michelle Obama. She showed up in glossy magazines everywhere, and inevitably had on an ensemble worth thousands or tens of thousands (even hundreds depending on the day's jewelry choice) of dollars!

The presentation could be fitting for a social role, but people saw it as ostentatious, and a glaring display of privilege and wealth, especially during a time when the economy was in downturn and many were feeling the pains of being in a recession.

Now, I know many in media describe Rogers as "glamorous" but there are many recorded instances of her dressed in a classic black suit and traditional button down shirt. So I asked her, beyond the actual clothes, to what did she attribute that glamorous perception. Is it personal style, natural presence, or some other intangible?

(Side note: when securing the interview with Rogers, her friend Melody Spann Cooper, owner of WVON, the largest urban talk radio station in Chicago and a *Pretty Powerful* woman in her own right, told me that Rogers was the kind of woman who could walk into a room with no makeup, do nothing more than run her fingers through her hair, show up in a pair of jeans and a t-shirt rocking a pair of stilettos and still command the attention of the entire room. Important to note that when I conveyed this antidote to Rogers, I neglected to include the stilettos and she was sure to add a "fabulous shoe" to the hypothetical jean and t-shirt ensemble.)

So what was this presence, this command that she couldn't seem to evade, whether in a basic button down, or couture gown? Rogers told me, "Early on, if someone didn't know anything about me they might be surprised at my comfort and confidence level in any environment. My grandma told me not to get intimidated by my surroundings and not to convince myself that anyone else mattered more than me and that I had as much to offer as anyone else. Whether you're there yet or not. Many times we discount ourselves before others even have a chance to. I come from a long line of strong women. No discounts. I have always entered all rooms with complete comfortability." This attitude is one that many of us only wish to have, and is the quintessential pretty power. Far beyond any physical appearance, having a genuine air of confidence, belief in oneself, is what makes any women pretty beyond words.

Rogers continued, "I'm a very self-confident person. No one can take that away from me. I'm also 5'10" so I can't exactly sneak into a room even if I wanted to. I always say I'm not going to change who I am, but I will work hard to make other people more comfortable. What does that mean? More often now, I make the first move. I introduce myself to people and initiate the conversation. I think about where I'm going and consider that in my choices. Yes, I'm fine in jeans and t-shirt sometimes, but I say we should all be allowed to salute who we are, we shouldn't be expected to fight that. Every day we should be progressing to be comfortable in our own skin and not so threatened by other people's choices."

Rogers followed with, "At the same time, I am sensitive to other people's perceptions. Don't lose yourself in the process, but try to reach out and meet people where they are comfortable. For example, if I'm behind a Fashion Fair counter I might say 'let's try this color together' so the client feels more included and comfortable. It's important to be true to yourself and be open and approachable. Now I find myself being more gregarious in groups, then I see people warm up to me and say, 'She's a girl, I'm a girl, she's just like me.' " Many of us are judged by our looks (whether you're seemingly *too* put together by the onlookers' standards, or not kempt enough.)

All of this begs an interesting question: should our brand as a woman be flexible enough to adapt and change to the comfort level of those around us, or is it more important to be true to who you are, and consequently present how you choose to present, in a way that's natural and truly reflective of you? Is it our role to appease the judges? To prove our acceptance to all those whom we encounter? It's a question we all have to answer for ourselves, while understanding what the implications of each answer are.

Rogers has always stayed true to herself. She has said

publically (and again, unapologetically), that she is "a businesswoman, not a politician." She is here to handle her business in the most adept way, and, for Rogers, that includes presenting in a "pretty" way. The brand is important to her (as, I argue, it should be for us all), and the brand largely includes the visual aspect. Rogers's interest in branding sent her further away from the good graces of the public when in an interview she stated, "We have the best brand on Earth: the Obama brand." There was an uproar at the idea of referring to and positioning President Obama as a "brand" (during that time often used only for products, not people, especially not *presidential* people). And not only that, but she had (was perceived as having) the nerve to include herself in this wonderful brand when referring to the president, first lady, and herself as a "we." Rogers's presentation and comfort with herself, though still very appealing (but more like that train wreck from which we can't look away) quickly turned into very negative attention.

As off-putting as Rogers was beginning to seem, no one could really express more than their personal bias because she was still excelling at her job. She supervised over 300 noteworthy events at the White House in just thirteen months, and then there was the very first state dinner of the Obama presidency.

Everyone remembers the November 24, 2009 state dinner debacle. The dinner, in honor of Indian Prime Minister Manmohan Singh, was well-done, well-coordinated, and ornately appropriate, but a little *too* well-attended. That evening is known for being crashed by a Virginia couple, Tareq and Michaele Salahi (winery owners and aspiring reality star celebrities) who thought gatecrashing in a beautiful, Indian-inspired gown and handsome tux was the perfect opportunity to get their thirty seconds of fame. These uninvited guests made it past security checkpoints (at least one requiring ID), into the White House complex, and managed to get close enough to actually meet President Obama! As you can imagine, the security breach and legal implications of this ridiculousness were a very serious matter and since the dinner and disaster happened under the watch of Rogers as social secretary, there was responsibility to be had. As you can imagine (or remember), there was intense scrutiny after that crash, and a few months later Rogers stepped down from her post. It was a joint decision between her and the president's office.

It's hard to leave anything on a bad note, but it's even harder to leave on a bad note that many use to define an otherwise untarnished legacy. It's also questionable that so much attention was paid to Rogers's aesthetic instead of the numerous accomplishments she's made as a business leader. If you do an Internet search for "Desirée Rogers Johnson Publishing" you're (unfortunately) likely to see more headlines about her wardrobe than of her professional achievements. You're likely to see the entry "Desirée Rogers re-energized *Ebony* magazine" right behind that of "Desirée Rogers steps out in leather pants, stiletto boots." And in articles about the crash, there's a high chance of talk about the dress she was wearing, its designer, and cost.

Robin Givhan, a fashion writer for *The Washington Post* has been quoted as saying, "The interest in Desirée Rogers's style began to overwhelm all the other things she was doing here." It's also been said that the one thing you never want to be in DC is a distraction, and Rogers had become a distraction. Rogers knows that her style and flair often distract people from her substance. Is the tradition-bound, conservative, misogynistic District at fault for an exceptional woman's aesthetic being turned into an obstacle, or was Rogers's pretty power (looks, education, capability, prestige) just too much?

Rogers shared, "Where I'm from you put on your finest in an effort to salute and honor your friends. I wore that gown [to the infamous White House dinner] to honor President Obama and First Lady Michelle Obama. [For me,] It's like attending a wedding, you make effort to look nice but you're not going to nor are you trying to look better than the bride! It was ridiculous. We need to stop it. Stop with the term 'dressing up.' Women should be able to express their personalities without criticism about who they are and what they represent. And it's not all about money. You can be (and I have been) completely stylish without wearing a single label. I suggest people get comfortable with other people's self-expression. Her choice shouldn't make you feel unbeautiful, unpretty, or unglamorous. To some extent we all get to choose what we look like every day. Stay in your lane and stop being so critical."

When we spoke, Rogers was completely candid in her reflection around our current social climate and how the dichotomy of a woman's aesthetic and professional power both intertwine and can be in conflict with one another, as we saw so clearly with her.

"In this country, our appearance (or people's perception of our appearance) is something you cannot escape. I spent years running from that reality. Now it's time to embrace ourselves. We put labels on people, 'she's pretty, she's not so pretty, she's glamorous, she's fabulous, she's plain,' and then we assign secondary meanings to those labels, 'she's approachable, she's not down to earth, she doesn't care about what I have to say or doesn't value a person like me.'

"Yes, some people are more glamorous than others. But let's not put that secondary meaning on everything. That's a mind game, and it's a costly one. It prohibits us from developing important relationships (often times with other women) and creates unnecessary boundaries that stifle growth and creativity. Let's not make ourselves afraid of each other, it's painful and counterproductive. Let's lift each other up in our varying forms instead of drawing lines of separation. I often hear women say to me after getting to know me 'Desirée, you're so down to earth!' The fact is I've always been down to earth."

Rogers shared in a different interview a little while ago, "At fifty, I have learned who I am. I am not going to change who I am. But I will work hard to make people feel more comfortable. For me to change who I am would be the end of my soul. But I can keep this in consideration as I am talking, socializing, and enjoying other people."

She shared in our time together for this conversation, "As far as the duality of being strong and stylish, I wouldn't say that I've been underestimated, but I've certainly been misunderstood. Of course you can be both, and women show that every day! But on truly reconciling power and pretty, we're still a work in progress." And until the day comes when fabulousness is no longer "lethal," I'd say I agree wholeheartedly!

CHAPTER 3

MEAN GIRLS

With insight from Meghan McCain

"I think women should be allowed to wear what they want. Period."

—MEGHAN MCCAIN

Meghan McCain, daughter of John McCain, is an author, columnist, and Fox News host (among other things) who is creating a strong media identity for herself outside of her father's professional ambitions. She has an opinion or two about the role aesthetics plays in a woman's professional narrative, and was gracious enough to meet me for coffee not too long ago to discuss the concept of *Pretty Powerful*. I was all too happy for her candidness in the conversation.

While reflecting on a few visible examples of the importance of aesthetics in the media (like it or not) she acknowledges the reality of it all, but just wishes culturally we could progress beyond it. She wishes we, as women, could just look the way we want to look and not be bothered for it. Almost immediately into the conversation, McCain shared, "I would love to go on TV without makeup on. I hate wearing makeup. I wish it would be socially accept-able, but so many things in politics and entertainment are just not. Looks have something to do with it."

Meghan is a very pretty woman. During our meeting she did not have any makeup on her face, and she still looked beautiful. Now I understand it might be annoying and uncomfortable to have to "look the part" all the time, but I wondered if there were ever instances where Meghan felt like it was a good thing that she is visually pleasing. To be honest, what she said took me off guard a bit and surprised me. "I don't think of myself that way. That's actually something that I really have to work on because the majority of my career is just how fat I am. A really big portion of my career, I've been fat shamed for a really long time. [I'm] by far the biggest woman at Fox, I'm pretty sure. I'm not skinny. I won't go on TV without wearing Spanx. It makes me feel more comfortable, and it really does smooth things out." It's amazing that McCain never thought about potential benefits around her appearance because she was too busy being fat shamed, but hearing her say it now I can understand. For her entire career, she struggled with negative comments and had anxiety around being one of the curvier women in television news.

Spanx, for those of you who are wondering about this age-old phenomenon in well-marketed skin, are body shaping undergarments and apparel (for men and women) that are designed specifically to tighten everything up. And for the record, I also wear them . . . regularly! I think Eva Longoria, or someone like her said, "Even if you're a size zero or a size sixteen, nobody doesn't benefit from Spanx." But I digress.

McCain continued, "Yeah, they're so uncomfortable. I hate it. I wish I didn't have to. I'd love to meet the woman who wakes up in the morning and is like, 'I'm gorgeous, I'm fabulous!' " She shares that as a woman in media, "I'm inundated with, 'You look terrible today, have you gained weight?' and 'What's going on with your pale legs,' that's the stuff that I get all day long." But I've also heard (when McCain and I have been on shows together), "McCain, you're smoking hot." "Where is McCain?" "She's a babe." "Put her in the leg chair." So she's heard comments meant to criticize and others meant to exalt, but I wanted to know if those more "affirming" comments also made McCain feel uncomfortable. She explained, "Fox and cable news in general, like CNN, MSNBC, and [the] whole industry is filled with gorgeous women. Everybody that walks into these buildings for the most part is aesthetically appealing, in one way or another. So for me, I agree with your premise [of *Pretty Powerful*] that it can help, but I think so much of it is what you have to say, right? I think if you have not done your research, and you're not smart, and you don't have something to say, it doesn't really matter how pretty you are."

We both know that ultimately, pleasing to the eye is not going to float you, but still, we take the measures to present the look that we know is expected and which will help us get the message across that we've been put on our platforms to get out. And we hope to do it in a way in which we can feel comfortable with the package that is unique to us, and not necessarily strive toward other people's expectations of what it should be.

I would welcome the day when we can all be as bare-faced and un-Spanxed as we want to be. It is just not the current climate, so that is why I wrote this book. I want to give women the insight around how to deal with this because this is the reality that unfortunately many (if not all) of us have to walk around in. What the hell do we do?

McCain feels that it is so stupid. She says, "The older I get, the less I care about attacks." But unfortunately, they still happen. Whether on a national platform, or in your day-to-day office environment, the people will talk, and will be loud about their opinion about any woman in a visible position. McCain's advice is to become more secure with yourself and "Don't read all the Tweets." (Or listen to that ladies' room gossip.) In reflection of her particular experience she says, "It's an unfortunate part of this industry, but I do think times are changing. I really do."

I think it is so important that McCain is open to talk about the body shaming aspect because a lot of women of all shapes and sizes deal with that. I will share with you an insecurity that I am always subconscious about—the size of my chest. It is something I struggled with as an adolescent, with them just being too big and taking center stage. Just getting comfortable with my body was and still is an intentional effort, and I think a lot of women from all walks of life struggle with it. Being a size fourteen separates McCain from people in the industry in many ways. She shares, "I'm not skinny, and I'm technically plus-size, but I am the average size of the American woman." Such a true point! McCain shares that she doesn't want to waste hours and hours of her life every day obsessing over her body. She tried in the past when she was much younger and it made her crazy. She says, "We work at a great network, I have a hot boyfriend, it's all fine. I do everything that one does to be on, make it work. I want to feel attractive."

Meghan is a blue-eyed, blonde-haired, beauty bombshell. And she is super smart, too, so I know that she must be cognizant of the fact that in many ways, she represents the classic American Beauty, but for McCain the body shaming is very real. When you're sitting on those couches on set, some of the angles are intense because viewers can see your whole body. McCain shares, "You can just see my whole side, you can see my legs. I've yet to be on any show that doesn't show your whole body unless you're in a satellite away."

I asked McCain to share what has been effective for her in her journey to be comfortable with herself and what can seem like constant judgement. She and many others think that although criticized, her size has also worked as an advantage for her. McCain is relatable and many women in many ways feel that credibility comes along with being a "real-sized" woman. There's a perspective of authenticity that comes along with that. She explains that "Honestly, it has ultimately helped my career, and my career launched because Laura Ingraham said that I was 'too plus-sized to be on TV.' It launched my career, and it made people start noticing me because people thought it was such an ugly thing to say. It was a terrible thing to say, so honestly, much like Ashley Graham [an American model known for being "plus-sized"]—I love her so much—she probably wouldn't be on the cover of *Sports Illustrated* if she were super skinny. She's a different type, and I feel like for me, people are so nasty to me about my weight, and I'm just like, there's some girl in Des Moines that can see me on TV, and [can] say I don't have to diet myself and Pilates myself into oblivion to go on TV and talk about politics. Because it should be about what you have to say, not your body. I would love to see more body [types] be on television. That more so than anything . . . all diversity of all kinds, I would love to see."

Laura Ingraham, talk radio personality and commentator who did a satirical piece commenting on McCain's weight and how it related to her professional opportunities, said on-air that McCain was too big to be on television and many people were so horrified by the remarks, that they started paying attention to McCain. They wanted to see what she looked like, and this is the really important part: they tuned in to see what she looked like but continued to watch because they wanted to know what she had to say. What she had to say was so compelling that McCain ended up landing a nationally syndicated talk radio show. This is a quintessential pretty power play. McCain took a tacky fat shaming comment and turned it on its head, landing high profile jobs in television news, best-selling books and talk radio.

I asked McCain if she were not on TV would she still make such an effort to be attractive and she shared a story about her mother and her grandmother: "Both [are] very high maintenance women, and I would say that in a loving way. My grandmother used to sleep in silk pajamas with peacock feathers. My mother was always wearing Chanel, and she doesn't leave the house without makeup. I think I was just raised around women where [presentation was important and] for the most part I like presenting at least some semblance of a put together self when I leave my house."

I can definitely relate to that! My grandmother was from the slums (didn't have a toilet in her house, she had an outhouse) but she still knew to look a certain way to go to the grocery store because you never know who you're going to meet and you never know to whom you're going to have to present. Specifically, my grandmother would get very upset with me if she picked me up from school for dance class and I was unkempt. Not only was I doing myself a disservice she would say, but I was also reflecting poorly on the family. When the world looked at me they were being informed about who I was and where I came from before I uttered a word. It was important to my grandmother that I be seen as a capable, respectful and disciplined young lady. Right or wrong, these assessments were absolutely taking place based on what I looked like and she didn't want be to be incorrectly branded.

My mother was very concerned and amazingly aware of the same thing. We struggled financially and my mother only shopped for me once a year when it was time to go back to school, so we made annual trips to discount retailers like Kmart, Walmart and when we could afford more, T.J. Maxx and Marshalls. While my classmates picked out their own clothes and wore any and every-thing, my mother was careful to dress me in khaki shorts, polo shirts, oxfords and penny loafers. Her decidedly preppy look was very purposeful. She told me that when I walked into the classroom she wanted each of my teachers to know that I was a serious, dedicated student who was there to learn. I found her approach annoying as a kid, but I see it as genius now. We lived on the west side of Char-lotte, I received free-lunches, and she was a single mom. My mother knew that consciously or subconsciously those factors created a lot of presumptions about what type of student I would be and what my teachers could expect of me. She was completely intentional about grabbing those presumptions by the throat and choking out any negative narratives before they could start. My mother ensured that I presented a certain way, because she wanted me to get a certain type of education. While there were many factors involved in my educational pursuit, my mother's packaging of me was no doubt one of them.

Similarly, McCain continued, "I think you've got to dress for the job you want and the life you want in a lot of ways and I don't mean you have to wear Armani, I just mean wash your hair, put on a little makeup if you want. Look like you take yourself seriously, and then I think the world will take you seriously. I used to, when I was much younger, when I interned at *Saturday Night Live* when I was in college, I used to dress ridiculous. I think I actually used to wear sweatpants to work. Not cute ones . . . old school sweatpants. I think it hurt me. It was a lesson I learned. You need to dress like you take your surroundings seriously. And, I don't mean expensive. I just mean, don't wear old gym sweatpants to work. But it's weird because the world is changing in so many different ways where, when I lived in LA my entire staff on the show I used to work on [was casual]. I was lucky if my [executive producer] came in with a shirt on."

McCain's story makes a few great points, with one being that taking your look "seriously" is very much regional and specific to your particular environment. Casual is a very "Los Angeles culture." I've lived in the South, I've lived on the West Coast, and now I live on the East Side in Manhattan, and McCain's right, dressing up on the West Coast is not closed-toe shoes. They do not believe in it, whereas in the South, that is literally a religion for us. They call it Sunday Best for a reason. Interestingly enough (and also based on regional norms), what's funny is that being from the South, my family asks you if you're sick when you're what they consider "too skinny" and small-sized, whereas in many industries, it is the standard. So it is interesting to me because what McCain presents, in my family, she's small. It might very well be what shaped my attitude toward this issue because that's how I was raised.

McCain wishes what we looked like simply didn't matter. It is an understandable take and one that could be incredibly appealing. McCain, like many women, hates wearing makeup and while she wishes she did not have to, she understands that in politics and entertainment looks have a lot to do with success. I submit that most industries far outside of politics and entertainment function in a way that makes looks matter a lot. Almost every industry including business, real estate, law, finance, and even technology companies rely heavily on branding and other image-conscious considerations. Looks matter in a lot of professional industries, despite many of our wishes that they didn't.

McCain goes on to say that she wishes to meet the woman who wakes up feeling gorgeous and fabulous. As much as she should feel that way, it would be utterly naive not to understand how difficult it is for women to feel beautiful in today's hypercritical society that's full of Internet trolls and the always-dreaded "Comments" section following online posts. But, what I am advocating is that we don't strive for an unattainable goal of someone else's standard of perfection. Instead, we should be the thoughtful curators of our own pretty power.

As for advice to navigate the existing world where looks continue to matter, McCain pushes for each of us to work to get more secure with ourselves regardless of the public's reaction. In her work to get more comfortable with herself and her size, McCain points out that times do seem to be changing. She's noticing and applauding more body diversity on air and in media marketing.

What Ingraham said about McCain is sadly unsurprising. I make that conclusion not in an effort to stereotype women as catty bitches, but a real evaluation that considers our history and current variables and how those things impact the way we treat each other. Ingraham was being petty, self-serving, and deliberate in trying to undermine McCain's professional ambition. And I greatly respect Ingraham, but I have to call it like I see it. Fortunately, McCain was undeterred and even more motivated to succeed in a television career. But the dynamic created by Ingraham's nasty comment often exists among women, particularly when they are operating in the same space and perceiving each other as direct or indirect competition.

I've had the great fortune to have some incredible women in law, politics, and media serve as amazing mentors for me throughout my career. That's why I'm happy to report that not all women succumb to the temptation of the woman-on-woman teardown. But those who do find themselves victim or aggressor of this pitiful dynamic are often caught up in the long, hurtful history of women.

Historically, women have had to battle for equality. We've had to march, protest, and file lawsuits for the right to vote, for equal treatment in the workplace, and not to be abused/assaulted. We've come a long way on gender equality issues, but throughout the world, and even in our beloved country, women continue to fight for complete equality on issues, including professional leadership opportunities, equal pay, and political representation. This continued marginalization does not make us victims. It makes us fighters. We have real world realities that tell us a false narrative that there only a few open spots for success if you're a woman (or any other marginalized group). That narrative can promote a token-like attitude that can say "only one of us will get to the top, so I need to take you out to ensure my own success and safety."

Many times we are not even aware of this scarcity-based mentality that can operate at our subconscious. Again, all women certainly don't buy into this sad mentality, but those who do are not necessarily primarily motivated by malice but instead are acting out of desperate fear that their security is being threatened by your ascent.

While working in news, I've experienced the shady comments, cold shoulders, or overt sabotage attempts from fellow women. While McCain was told she was "too big to be on television", I've been told I was too young, too strong in my opinions, or, my favorite, "but she's black!" The comment about my race didn't seem like the crude racist comment that it plainly was when it came out of the woman's mouth, instead it was her desperate cry to distinguish herself from me so that the network decision-makers clearly understood that my presence was different than hers, thus her position was still needed. Wow. I can't help but wonder if Ingraham consciously or subconsciously saw McCain broaching "her territory" as a beautiful blonde conservative commentator and was so threatened that she felt the need to make the nasty size comment in an effort to "take her out."

This is why it's critically important for women to stop buying into the false narrative that only "one" of us can succeed at a time. Men do not generally do this to each other. That's not to say that men aren't competitive with each other because they are, but they are not burdened by a hurtful history that has attempted to sideline their efforts at leadership, financial independence, and power. Because women have seen those attempts thwarted for years and have seen only small numbers of us escape those marginalization efforts, we tend to be vulnerable to the unintended (or perhaps intended) consequences of being hostile toward each other.

Studies show that women threatened by social or professional exclusion will reject each other first. In the essay "Women Who Hate Other Women: The Psychological Root of Snarky," Dr. Seth Meyers concludes that women he's seen clinically over the years reported far greater anxiety in the appearance department than men. Specifically, Meyers cites greater pressure from men and the media to fit into certain physical norms and body types. The notions of thinness and unattainable beauty ideals grow so intimidating that we often turn on each other. He goes on to tell of a 2012 study from Shannon Snapp and her colleagues which found that young women with high family support and low levels of perceived sociocultural pressure from family, friends, and the media regarding the achievement of a "thin and beautiful" ideal had a more positive body image.

Meyers's analysis is helpful in trying to understand

why so many women resort to such nasty behavior toward one another. But there is no excuse, and as so many have shown through example there is plenty of room for all of us to flourish in our chosen professions. Therefore, we should do ourselves and each other a favor and support our individual and collective efforts to find success. Contrary to popular opinion we are not direct threats to each other, so we must reject that stale narrative. Instead we should embrace the truth that another woman's success only broadens the palette and appetite for more of us to build with her, expand the foundations created before us, and ultimately be seen as the standard bearers in every industry.

Not possessing the mainstream media's ideal body type has undoubtedly played a large role in McCain's daily navigation of her industry, and her need to rely on herself (her own strong mindset and credibility) to continue to feel comfortable with her physical aesthetic. As a woman of color, particularly a black woman, it has also been difficult to feel confident in my aesthetic when so many of the messages the world receives about what's "pretty" is based on a Eurocentric aesthetic. This fact is responsible for generations of women struggling to find pride in their darker complexions, textured hair, or brown eyes. While there is certainly no monolithic look for all women of color or all white women, there are very real beauty standards in the world and in our country.

My past experiences have affirmed that my look was commercially palatable, but as a youth, the affirmation was often couched in the condition that I'm "pretty for a black girl." It was many years later that I understood this as a qualifier to my look, and ultimately a limit to my commercial appeal. When I was a commercial actress, there were certain roles that my agent would not send me out for because they were not considering "ethnic" talent. As I learned more about the advertising world, I understood that they were marketing to target audiences and therefore implementing a strategic business plan that just happened to come across as discriminatory. What advertisers and other marketing professionals continuously fail to realize is that while they are executing a business plan, they are also the definers of beauty standards. When they limit the types of people they use in their campaigns, they also are creating and feeding a system that makes it very difficult for those of us outside their projected images to be seen as or feel pretty.

And this goes for anyone who finds herself outside the mainstream projection of beauty, from skin color, to hair texture, to body size, or anything else. It is critical that in the journey toward pretty power, each of us relies on our own ideas and comfort levels to define our aesthetic goals, and give little power to those who do all they can to undermine it.

CHAPTER 4

PRETTY POLITICS

With insight from Monica Crowley

> *"You want to inspire confidence in the way you look."*
>
> —MONICA CROWLEY

Monica Crowley and I met doing television together years ago, and developed a closer relationship appearing as debate partners weekly on the twenty season run, highest viewed Fox News Channel cable television series *The O'Reilly Factor*. Anyone who knows (or Googles) Crowley is going to know immediately that she is a stunningly beautiful woman. She can be seen on television every single day, ready with analysis of the biggest political headlines and looking gorgeous.

But long before her career was in front of the camera, she operated with thoughtfulness, range, and authenticity around her look. Whether working as an entry-level political operative, a college lecturer, or even in her personal life, Crowley reminds us that being concerned with your aesthetic presentation isn't reserved for women or men who are seen on the screen. Make no mistake about it: intention around your appearance and how it impacts your professional trajectory is not exclusive to those on camera.

Crowley's first job out of college was actually quite an extraordinary one. Going into her senior year at Colgate University, she read one of President Nixon's foreign policy books, and it so moved her, so educated her, so enlightened her, that it had a huge impact on the way she thought about the world, America's place in it, and what she wanted to do with the rest of her life. She was so moved that she sat down and wrote him a letter. It didn't even occur to her that she was writing to a former president of the United States. She just felt compelled to let that particular author know that he had changed her life with a single book. So, she wrote him a letter, kind of forgot about it, and about a month later she went to her mailbox and there was a handwritten note from the former president in her mailbox. At the end of that note, he invited Crowley to come in and talk to him, which she did. That conversation led to a full-time job offer to join the office as a foreign policy assistant once she graduated college.

At the young age of twenty-two years old, Crowley's first job was working with the former president of the United States. Now let's take a sidebar here. Much of what we discuss in this chapter as it relates to the "pretty" part of *Pretty Powerful* is a dialogue that when considering your aesthetic, it is important to understand your environment and audience (in both your personal and professional life), and to remain authentic and classy in the process. It is very clear that Crowley has the credibility part down pat, and has from a young age.

After securing the interview of a lifetime—mid-August 1989—and determining it was real and not one of her friends playing a joke on her, Crowley unapologetically confesses that she immediately started to think about what she was going to wear. Crowley explains, "Because what does a twenty-one, twenty-two year old young adult wear to see a former president of the United States? I immediately was nervous." Some may scoff at her immediate concern about what she looked like, but it signals that she understood a very important reality. What you look like communicates a great deal about who you are and what you represent.

Crowley consulted with her mom and the consensus was, "You meet a former president in a dark navy blue suit. You're not going to take a lot of license or at least I didn't think at the time to take a lot of license with creativity." She identified the look as "very typically Republican conservative," and added, "I wasn't going to go in meeting him looking like Madonna or Beyoncé obviously." A pointed distinction between the hypersexual and overly glamorous appearance of the two pop stars, versus what she deemed a necessity to appear as a conservative, young, professional woman. When probed further, she expressed that part of that decision was because she was representing the values of the conservative party, but also because she wanted very much to be taken seriously as a young woman in a male-dominated and older work environment. Crowley shared her feeling that, "It was being thrust into a very adult, very professional world immediately, so I would say that was baptism by fire in a lot of ways, which had nothing to do with gender per se, because I was immediately thrust into a world where I was going to the White House and I was meeting with heads of state at a very young age." So she went to Ann Taylor and bought a navy blue, button down skirt suit and "A new pair of navy blue, black pumps, typically Republican conservative" and landed the job!

Crowley's decision to write to a former U.S. president was a complete power play. She had no connection to this man, was an undergraduate student with no real "qualifications" or presumption of authority, yet she felt compelled to reach out to Richard Nixon and tell him how much he'd impacted her life. She did so with no real expectation of a response and certainly no particular end goal in mind. But she was confident enough to put her thoughts out into the universe and be open to what came back to her. What came back was the opportunity of a lifetime and a complete change of course to her professional trajectory.

When retelling the story, she shared, "It sort of didn't even occur to me that I was writing to a former president of the United States." That sounds like blind optimism, and sometimes that is the best kind. Many times we psych ourselves out of opportunities before they can even materialize because we tell ourselves destructive false narratives; "He/she doesn't know who I am," "They'll never even read this," "I'm not experienced enough to be considered for this role," "They probably get a million emails and phone calls, they'll never respond to me, I'm just a random person."

If Crowley had told herself any of those negative false narratives she would never have had the courage to send her letter to President Nixon and would likely not be enjoying the incredible success she now has. The lesson is simple: If you're thinking about putting yourself out there, just do it. Who cares if nothing comes of your effort? What have you lost? Nothing, yet you create an opportunity to gain the world.

In my professional journey I've heard "no" (or worse yet, been ignored with no response at all) hundreds of times. When I decided to transition from practicing law to a career in media, I set a goal for myself to make five attempts to secure a media opportunity every day. That meant emails, telephone calls, Tweets, biography and headshot mailings, and they were almost always "cold" (i.e. to people who I didn't know and certainly didn't know me). Most of the time I never heard one word back from them. Occasionally, I was given a courteous, "No, thank you." The key is knowing that you only need one "yes."

Eventually I received a "yes" and I was afforded the opportunity to pursue my dream. You don't have to take my word for it, just ask Crowley: one "yes" can literally change your life. She sent a letter of admiration and ended up with a job, her first job at that, being with a former president of the United States. That is an ultimate power play.

At the time Crowley started her position, President Nixon was based in New Jersey. In the early '90s, President George H. W. Bush was in office, so once in a while when President Nixon would write him a long memo of advice, he didn't want to send it by mail or FedEx or anything. He wanted it hand delivered, so he would send Crowley down to the White House.

She brilliantly pointed out that with this role, she would be working as a public servant, and as such she wanted to reflect respect for the public pocketbook. Her look needed to convey an understanding and appreciation of the fiscal responsibility she had to the community. That's not to say that anyone working in the public sector needs to look inexpensive or less put-together, but it's the acknowledgement that when you work on behalf of the public and the public is paying you, you need to have an awareness of that fact reflected in your appearance. Crowley astutely articulates that visual reflection ensured her credibility to the public and that would continue to serve her throughout her career.

Crowley says, "[at that time] you want to inspire confidence in the way you look to the whole political world, and it still holds true today—although people, especially women, are taking a little more freedom in terms of how they dress and how they present themselves. But at that time, it was a very buttoned-down universe." Crowley felt enormous responsibility for presenting a strong conservative image because what she was presenting to the world was on behalf of the former president of the United States. She wanted to represent Nixon well and be responsible about it.

On an average day when, say it was just four of them in the office—the president, and his very small staff—Crowley says, "I might go to work in a long sleeve blouse—short sleeve blouse in the summer—a skirt, and a heel. Maybe a kitten heel, something like that. When I knew he was having an important guest in the office—former President Ronald Reagan came to see him now and again then—I would step it up and that would mean a little more pulled together, a little more tailored, but also a little better quality." Crowley continued, "I took extra care, so a lot of times it was skirt suits, some pants suits once in a while, but mostly skirt suits and dresses, sometimes blouses with skirts and so on. Always conservative. I knew that if he had important guests coming in to the office, I would always step up my game one more step or have an extra special dress or extra special suit ready to go that was better quality—which still holds true today, but it was always erring on the conservative side."

Crowley shared that to the extent that she could afford it at the time, "I would pay a little more for expensive quality [sometimes] because I think that for me that brings more confidence when I know that I'm dressed well." And she thinks that individual affordability should be the barometer. No matter what one's income scale is, she says, "Dressing well doesn't have to be expensive necessarily, it has to be well tailored. So you can get a dress at T. J. Maxx or Marshalls. I do it all the time. If it doesn't fit perfectly, take it to a good tailor and have them nip it or shorten it or whatever they need to do. An inexpensive dress can look fantastic if it fits you well." This is such a great note, that with the help of a good tailor and consistent eye, even if you purchase your clothing from bargain stores or even receive them second-hand, it's not about the designer or label, it's about the two Fs: fit and fabric. As long as the fit and fabric are on point, you'll have an easy time looking polished, professional, and attractive.

I know a lot about Crowley's professional pursuits— Fox News analyst, columnist, bestselling author, and editor—and how those roles translate into her thoughts about her aesthetic presentation, but at some point in her description of her conservative wardrobe choices at the White House, I got curious and wanted to get a glimpse into Crowley's personal life as a young twenty-something woman, living life, having fun, dating, socializing with her girlfriends, versus her serious, professional, political business working for a president. I asked her if she had a uniform, so to speak, and if her choices around how she presented to the world were different in her personal, real life.

Crowley shared, "Sure, absolutely. And I think anybody who keeps the same uniform in professional life and private life is making a big mistake and missing out on a lot of fun because in your personal/private life you have more freedom to dress perhaps more expressively in connection to who you are, who you authentically are. So yeah, [in] my downtime, if I were going on a date that would be more of a dress, maybe with a sexier edge to it, nothing too crazy, I was raised a good girl!"

Crowley continues, "Everything in moderation, but you have a little more freedom when you're going out with your friends. So out with friends would be a cute top and jeans, or a sundress. You're going out on a date, a sundress, something that was a little less constrictive than the suits, blouses, and dresses that I was wearing in my professional life."

I appreciate the conservative nature that Crowley wanted to exhibit in her professional life, but some may not associate a traditionally conservative aesthetic with femininity, and that could be off-putting for those women who love to show theirs. I asked Crowley to tell me where femininity, if at all it, fit into her scheme and her look.

For Crowley, femininity was paramount, "Always. Always and forever. Always. And I am such a strong believer and supporter of women who are intelligent, educated, accomplished, strong, as well as being feminine. Everyone has their own look and their own path so if you don't choose that path or naturally you are not feminine or you're more of a 'tomboy,' God bless you, stay true to who you are. Authenticity is the key. Authenticity feeds confidence. If you are trying to be something you're not, you're not going to come off as authentic and that will chip away at your confidence in whatever context you happen to be in. So be true to yourself. Now for me, I was always a girly girl. I was always raised with the Barbie dolls. I was always pink everything. My bedrooms were pink, my shag rug growing up was pink. My dresses were pink growing up. I loved dolls. I was a girly girl and I'm still a girly girl. So to be true to that I always made sure that the clothes that I chose had a feminine edge to them. Even the suits, the Ann Taylor suits in the early '90s. The big thing was a little shoulder pad with a little peaked shoulder. I made sure I always had that because it cut the masculine edge of the suit. I always made sure that I had something going on that told the world I was a woman and proud of it. Whether that was a heel, or stiletto heel with a pantsuit, or whether that was jewelry; and makeup for me was always big."

I was curious how Crowley balanced her love of makeup with working in a conservative environment. She explains, "I have always loved makeup. Hair and makeup. In fact, growing up I always got all of the fashion magazines. *Vogue, Harper's Bazaar, Elle*, and I would immediately go to the beauty pages. The fashion pages came second. The beauty pages always came first. I loved to see makeup artists' work. I loved to see the transformation that they could do on any face in the world. They could metamorphize it into something completely different. I remember reading about the great, late makeup artist Kevyn Aucoin who could turn [one] celebrity's face into a completely different celebrity's face. The transformation to me is miraculous, so I've always loved makeup and have always played with makeup in my professional life. Now at Fox obviously we have pros who do it for us every day. You do yours and you do it beautifully, but I always go into a makeup artist knowing what I want, encouraging them to do what I want."

Speaking of her work at Fox, I asked Crowley about what factors into her thoughts when deciding how she wants to look for a particular segment or show in the sense of the tone, and the substance of what she is going to be speaking about. She replied, "I think if you are doing a morning show, it's a little lighter of an environment, less intense, less restrictive, even when you're talking about very serious issues . . . the time of day makes a difference. I wouldn't go on a morning show in a cocktail dress, for example, because it's a morning show. But I would take more license to dress in a more fun color or maybe a shorter skirt or maybe something a little more optimistic, bubbly, and sunny because it's the start of everybody's day. When I'm doing primetime it's a different calculation. I factor into my wardrobe and the look that I'd like to have more confidence going into a primetime show because there are more eyeballs on you, perhaps discussing more serious topics, and so then I might reach for a jacket that has shoulder pad in it, that cuts a cleaner, stronger line, which gives me more confidence, which I am then able to project on television. For special events, for example, say election night, I might reach for something more conservative because it is election night and there is more gravitas that goes along with that. It is all about two things: honestly representing who I am in terms of confidence, my experience, my accomplishments, my femininity, [and] representing the brand." She continues, "When you're dealing in a visual medium, I think you have a responsibility to your employees as well as to yourself for your own self-respect to present yourself in a pulled together, professional, polished way." And adds, "[Same as when] I was working for President Nixon, I always felt when I got dressed every morning that I was presenting to the world, not just my authentic self, but I was representing him as well."

I have the feeling in my gut that Crowley would look very similar to how she looks on television if she were in a classroom right now. She confirms, "And that is true, because I care about what I look like. I care about the image I present to the world, but frankly, I also just want to know that I look attractive every day and I don't think there's anything wrong with that—man or woman. I think taking pride in the way you look, maximizing what you have, being proud, and relishing your look no matter what it is, owning it, having it as your authentic image; owning it and embracing it I think is a beautiful thing. I think life is too short to constantly be fighting your body whether it's with weight or any other issue. Yes, we all want to be healthy. I'm a big believer in exercise and eating healthy. I'm also a big believer in you never know what's going to hit you tomorrow. You should enjoy your life, so have that brownie. Again, everything in moderation, but have that ice cream, have that brownie. And again, be healthy in your choices. I think if you have the self-confidence, self-esteem—which takes a lot of people a lot of work to get there—take pride in who you are, and take pride in your appearance. I don't see anything wrong with that whatsoever. We're in a place now in the twenty-first century where it's no longer an either/or. You don't have to be unattractive to be taken seriously. You can have both. It gets to the point of confidence, because if you're confident in your education, your background, your accomplishments, your experience, that confidence will come through in how you project yourself to the world. A little mascara is not going to detract from your seriousness of purpose."

Crowley spends time making important points about range and adjusting the narrative you should convey in certain environments while still being authentic to yourself. What she wears in her personal life and what she wears in her professional life are understandably different, but she points out that while she took more liberties in her personal style, she still didn't get "too crazy." This is a personal choice, but especially important in today's society where Instagram, Facebook, and Snapchat allow current and potential employers, clients, and the entire world to see so much of our personal lives, and those moments are captured forever.

The thought of perception following you started a conversation between us about how women choose to express themselves through clothing and physical appearance. I specifically wanted to know Crowley's thoughts on the line between women "appropriately" utilizing their femininity and what some might consider classless or something that skirts the line—pun intended—of hyper-sexuality.

Crowley shares, "I will tell you, some of the moments that made me most proud are when I'm in a public environment, say signing my book, like at a book signing, or walking down the street in Manhattan, or if I'm at a restaurant, and people who watch Fox News recognize me and approach me, some of my proudest moments are [with] parents. [Once] at a book signing, a mother had her young daughter with her who must have been about seven or eight years old, and she took her by the hand, and the daughter was very shy meeting me because she recognized me from television, and she got all shy, and her mother took my hand and squeezed it, and said, 'I wanted to bring my daughter here today to meet you in person because you are such an extraordinary role model for her,' and I said, 'Thank you so much.' And she said, 'No, I really want to let you know why you are a role model for her, because you are strong, you are strong in your opinions, you are not shy about expressing them, you saw your education through to the end, you had the perseverance to do that, you have built a very successful career, and you have never compromised your principles,' and then she said, 'And you always show up on the air dressed like a lady.' And she said that to me, and it's not the first time, and it wasn't the last time I've heard that. There are a lot of women who feel that the only way perhaps that they can get ahead is by flashing some flesh. I was always raised to be a lady by my mother who, when I was nine and my sister was seven, my father left and she had to be mother and father to the two of us. And boy she cracked that whip. She 'raised two ladies,' she is proud to say. And I think when you work in any industry, any profession it doesn't have to be on television, any profession, you speak more and with more authority and more power when you are dressed like a lady. That doesn't mean don't take some creative license with and have some fun with your personality but in terms of flashing flesh, in terms of too tight, or dressed inappropriately in the workplace, I think it takes away from your power. I think it detracts from what you have to say as a professional and as a human being because people are just seeing that and they're not listening to you. They are more distracted by what you are putting on display than who you are as a person, what you have accomplished, what you have to say and do in the world. So when she said that to me and her little girl beamed at me, it made it all worthwhile. I think a lot of women, especially young women feel that perhaps I have to dress this way to compete with other women in my industry or this is what they're showing in the pages of *Vogue* or any of the women's magazines, so I have to dress this way. No, you don't. Again, it's all about authenticity. Stay true to yourself, but class trumps everything else. And remember in life, whether it is clear in your relationships, in your friendships, in life this is a marathon, not a sprint. Don't go for the shortsighted gain of, if I flash a little flesh, I'm going to get this job or that job, or the male boss is going to look at me differently and give me this promotion; just remember self-respect at the end of the day trumps everything."

CHAPTER 5

FREE ENTERPRISE

With Insight from Janice Bryant Howroyd

"Everything Matters! Give smart attention to everything and you'll actually save time, money, and other resources."
—JANICE BRYANT HOWROYD

That's a strong proclamation, but one that's entirely true! There's no doubt that Janice Bryant Howroyd is a woman of detail, and it was (and still is) her attention to detail in *everything* that gave her start as a small business owner, and ultimately propelled her to the achievement of being the first African American woman to own and operate a billion-dollar business.

Entrepreneur, businesswoman, author, educator, ambassador, and Presidential Special Appointee of President Obama, Howroyd is the founder and CEO of ACT-1 Group, the largest certified woman-minority-owned staffing agency in the United States. The Torrance,

California, based, full-service agency finds both temporary and direct-hire placements for administrative and
technical personnel. The agency has over seventy office
locations nationwide, and won recognition as the 2015
Staffing Industry Analyst Best Staffing Firms to Work For,
among other accolades throughout its over 40 years of
existence.

"Everything Matters" is one of the values Howroyd
impresses upon ACT-1's more than 65,000 temporary
employees and more than 300 direct employees nationwide. In a blog post titled "Seven Keys to Starting" she
explains, "We teach it with an exclamation mark because
it's just that critical to us." That sentiment is one I firmly
believe in, and seems to be a consistent belief among the
many strong, driven, successful women I'm blessed to know
(many of whom were gracious enough to share their stories
and philosophies for *Pretty Powerful*). From a woman's
preparedness, to her presentation, everything *does* matter.
And we do ourselves a disservice if every aspect of both is
not treated as a critical detail in our ascent to success.

Howroyd is no stranger to being prepared for any
situation. She was groomed for preparedness even before
founding ACT-1 in 1978. Howroyd was born in the small
town of Tarboro, North Carolina in 1953 and grew up
as one of eleven children in her family. She was raised in
a town of few opportunities, in a time of challenge, but
her parents instilled in her the values of being prepared,
staying focused, and remaining determined to be able to
achieve a life of opportunity. Throughout her schooling,
Howroyd's parents taught her that she had to be twice as
smart as others to be successful in life.

When it came time to enter high school, she was sent to

the town's all-white school during the early stages of the town's desegregation efforts. She (like many other brave African American students taking part in this change) was immediately challenged. She remembers that one of her teachers openly remarked and taught that people of African descent were only good for slave labor and affirmative action was wrong for the country.

On so many days, Howroyd came home full of concern, disappointment, and frustration, but on those days, her parents reminded her of her mental strength, and did something that many parents may not have had the courage to do. They told her she was the one who would make her own decision about whether or not to return. And each day, she did.

That determination, and the consistent encouragement from her parents were no doubt the foundations that built her character and gave her the substance required to be the *Pretty Powerful* woman she's known to be today. She also attributes much of her substance to faith.

Reflecting back in a BET Women's History Month interview years ago, Howroyd shared that "divine intervention" is what inspired her to begin her business. Awhile after graduating from North Carolina A&T University, she went to Los Angeles, California, to visit with her sister. As the visit was nearing an end, she felt more and more strongly that she didn't want to return home to the east, but she needed a way to make a living for herself if she was going to be able to make the permanent move to Southern California. At that time (1976), her sister's husband was working at *Billboard*, a large music industry corporation, and he offered her a job in his office.

Howroyd (of course, having been taught long ago how

to recognize and jump on the right opportunity) took the job. Not only did she "take the job," but she dove in and took real ownership of her role instead of just sitting back, relaxing, and leaning on the family connection. She took the job and put in hard work to learn the company and make improvements to existing processes. She also showed up, presenting well and ready to work and gained trust as a confident employee. Then, one time when Howroyd's brother-in-law was out of the country for a business trip, she took initiative to hire necessary staff. When he returned home, he was thoroughly impressed with what Howroyd had done. He "thought [she] was a genius, and encouraged [her] to assist a friend who needed to hire several employees too." All of Howroyd's experience to that point taught her not to shy away from the additional opportunity, so she took it, tackled it, and did a great job for her brother-in-law's friend as well. Her work was so strong, that she was encouraged to go into business for herself.

In 1978, Howroyd started her staffing company in an office in Beverly Hills. She explains that she built her business on two principles: "the WOMB method and the notion of keeping the humanity in Human Resources." The letters in WOMB represent Word of Mouth, Brother! Howroyd made a promise to companies that she would only provide them with qualified employees, or return any payment they'd already made. With this approach, the ACT-1 reputation reflected a gold standard, spread without much formal advertising, and had earned about $10 million within a few years. She has been quoted as saying, "Never compromise who you are personally to become who you wish to be professionally. That means you only do business with a company you'd send a relative to, and you look to work with companies you can get repeat business from. That's how I measure success." With gained experience, faith, a mission, and herself as the sole employee, a longstanding empire was born.

She admits that she also understands previous "jobs and trials along the way" helped her throughout her journey of building experience and being ready, but ultimately, a need and a vision are what has gotten her to a place on the Forbes' list of America's Richest Self-Made Women.

A person's vision, determination, and upbringing are often the main ingredients in the ascent to being a powerful woman. Building yourself up to be a woman of substance through learning, life experiences, and testing your limits, combined with the encouragement and teachings of those around you make it hard to stop anyone from being able to achieve anything she sets her mind to achieve.

My mother grew up in a two-room house—with an outhouse serving as a bathroom—in the heart of the deeply segregated South in small town Amite, Louisiana. The elementary and middle schools she attended were all-black schools. She was not allowed to go to an integrated school until she reached high school.

Her father, my grandfather, did not graduate from high school. He actually had a fourth-grade education. My grandfather had to drop out of school to help his parents with the farming duties. My grandmother graduated from high school, and immediately went on to work as a domestic—a maid for the wealthy whites in the town. She made a living cooking and cleaning their houses, and rearing their children.

My grandfather decided, although he was not formally educated, that he wanted more control over his way of life. He had a very entrepreneurial spirit. My grandfather did anything he could get his hands on to supplement income for his family, from working as a carpenter building homes, to carrying and bagging food for cows and horses at a feed meal factory, a hugely popular industry in south Louisiana at that time. On top of this, he worked part-time as a barber where he cut hair in the living room of their two-room home.

So coming from the background where my grandfather had no formal education, where he had to work his fingers to the bone—manual labor was his way of life to provide for his family—and then my grandmother not having any advanced education and working as a maid her entire life, my mother observed those two paths and rejected them as anything she wanted for her own life.

While my mother did not complete her formal education either, she graduated from high school in three years at age sixteen. She started college at Texas Southern University, a historically black college in Houston. She studied through her sophomore year there where she intended on declaring as a business major. When she went to her business class in her sophomore year, her teacher said, "If you do everything right, you interview well, you get good grades, you will eventually earn up to $50,000 a year." For my mother at that time, we are talking about 1979, she decided that that was nowhere near enough money for the basic lifestyle she wanted to live. In retrospect, it's funny because it was not that low, but it was low to her.

She had learned the value of entrepreneurship from her father which meant having your own, and not working for people because people will always only pay you but so much, but when you work for yourself, you set the terms and you control your own financial destiny. That was what my grandfather taught her. And she believed in it. She was going to be a business owner.

So, she decided to leave college and immediately start working in a managerial position. The next day she walked to the local Popeye's Fried Chicken fast food franchise and was hired as an assistant manager. She worked her way up eventually to regional manager of those franchises.

After working as a manager for some time, my mother decided it was time for her to get her own business going. She would use the managerial skills that she honed in fast food management positions to open her own beauty salon. The only catch was she did not know how to style hair. But that did not stop her from sending herself to beauty school with the money she earned on her job and Federal Pell Grants.

My mother completed beauty school in half the time it traditionally takes, and never for one day worked for any other salon. She hung a shingle and opened her own salon right out of beauty school—which everyone said she was crazy to do but she did it. Within a year, she was making a six-figure salary. From there she went on to open another location of her beauty salon. It became a chain of sorts. Then she opened day care facilities. She had two of those at one time. She took all the money she earned from those proceeds and bought tractor-trailers, cash outright. She had a small fleet. At one time, she had up to four trailers and four trucks. She was able to run—as a single woman by herself—a small tractor-trailer business out of Charlotte, North Carolina, where she would distribute goods up and down the East Coast.

Making your own way as an entrepreneur and business owner is something that Howroyd, my mother, and so many other women (me and many of you, too), have done by being able to harness experiences and a natural drive toward being *Pretty Powerful* women.

In fact, women business owners are growing at an unprecedented pace in the United States. African American businesswomen, specifically, are the second fastest-growing group of entrepreneurs, after Latina women. *Fortune* reports that the number of businesses owned by African American women grew 322 percent from 1997 to 2015, "making black females the fastest growing group of entrepreneurs in the U.S." An article in *Fortune*'s Leadership series shares the statistics that, overall, the number of women-owned businesses grew by 74 percent between 1997 and 2015—a rate that's 1.5 times the national average, according to the "2015 State of Women-Owned Businesses Report" commissioned by American Express Open.

According to statistics, women now own 30 percent of all businesses in the U.S. (estimated at approximately 9.4 million firms), and African American women control 14 percent of these companies, or an estimated 1.3 million businesses. Based on report findings, that figure is larger than the total number of firms owned by all minority women in 1997.

Co-founder and CEO of The U.S. Women's Chamber of Commerce, Margot Dorfman has seen a recent increase in membership from black women entrepreneurs, attributing the rise in women-owned firms to "lack of fair pay, fair promotion, and family-friendly policies found in corporate America." She adds, "With all of the negative factors that women face [it's] not surprising that they have chosen to invest in themselves."

The entrepreneur's playground has expanded considerably for all women since the times when my mother, Howroyd, and other trailblazers crafted and executed their powerful visions. By running thriving businesses, they and many of you are adding hundreds and thousands of jobs to our economy and serving as models for others. As players and role models in the business space, there is no question that presentation is (and absolutely should be) a serious consideration right along with that all important preparation. The way a leader or employee (in the business arena or otherwise) shows up, speaks, carries her (or him)self, dresses, and all other visually noticeable aspects of a person makes a marked difference in their success.

As a potential employee, the only way you're making it into that interview in the first place is after your qualifications have been deemed great enough for people to spend their time on you in a further conversation. Most employers agree that once you're in that door, appearance becomes the biggest point of consideration for moving forward; the substance has already been vetted. Appearance means overall all physical presentation: wardrobe, personal grooming, nonverbal communications, and general demeanor. Appearance is in no way limited to traditional concepts of beauty or conventional prettiness. Many women incorrectly determine that they don't fit mainstream society's definition of "pretty," thus these women disregard the appearance element of the equation all together. Often the conclusion they reach is that being perceived as "beautiful" simply wasn't a card they were dealt, therefore they should focus entirely on the other elements that they possess, like intelligence or a strong work ethic. I reject this conclusion as short sighted. Certainly some women are born with more natural beauty than others, but this fact alone does not disqualify any woman from deciding to make a concerted effort to maximize or improve upon her appearance (as broadly defined above) as a savvy business strategy. When Howroyd preaches attention to detail in everything, the decision made around one's appearance is a perfect example of how broadly she intended that statement.

Howroyd takes her role as a staffing agency CEO to a level where she doesn't just find placements for highly qualified people, but she also educates them on being professionals who can be trusted to get the job done, and to represent a company well. Her reputation is always on the line, so it's a double investment! She uses education to teach the best ways to present as an interviewee. You can even find "Dos" and "Don'ts" for effective interviewing listed on the ACT-1 website: Smile and have a firm handshake. Be sure to look the employer in the eye when talking to him/her. Be conscience of your body posture as well. An upright, sturdy appearance gives the impression of confidence. The first tip is all about presentation, with nothing about the mental and experiential preparedness.

In similar fashion, entrepreneurs must secure opportunities to be "interviewed" prior to getting that business off the ground. Countless hopeful business leaders have great plans and smart offerings, but who's going to fund them? A good idea without the right backers will fall flat, and trust me: if a potential investor has agreed to a pitch meeting, it's because they already see merit in the business idea . . . what they want to learn more about is the person attached to the idea. How do they present? Are they articulate? Is there an air of capability? What are her wardrobe choices communicating? Everything is being assessed, and a decision will never be made before the full package is right in the eyes of whomever is making the inescapable judgement.

And once a business owner has made it to public notice, the media is all too ready to jump in and scrutinize. Stories in the media increase transparency, hold those spotlighted accountable, and provide inspiration to other entrepreneurial onlookers. Today's public has an insatiable appetite for information, and they don't just want to know what you do, they want to know what you look like doing it. It can make or break your reputation. Businesswomen like Janice Bryant Howroyd are headlined in the media and become part of the "celebrity" world just because of the empires they've built.

The more you are in the headlines, the more other opportunities present themselves, and then you have to be prepared and well-presented for any crowd. Howroyd became deeply immersed in her industry (as business leaders should), and started to connect the dots to broader services. Over the years, she has invested millions in creating the staffing industry's most advanced technology and talent platform. The platform serves many diverse industries worldwide, from energy, to utilities, to broadband communication. ACT-1 was also responsible for creating an electronic time card that companies can use to track temporary employee capacity effectively. These expansions and others have increased her understanding of global markets and trends, and made her a highly sought after ambassador and speaker on global business issues. Even former President Barack Obama took note and appointed Howroyd (a proud HBCU alumna) to serve on the Board of Advisors for the White House Initiative on Historically Black Colleges and Universities (HBCUs). The purpose of the Board was to advise the president and the secretary of education on methods, programs, and strategies to strengthen HBCUs, and make recommendations on how to increase the private sector role in ensuring the long-term viability and enhancement of these institutions.

In a recent blog post, Howroyd stated, "Goals may be seeded from wishes and ideals, but they require strategies to be realized. Be very clear and concise in identifying your goals; then, be even more critical and precise in defining your strategies. Goals, without strategies, are wasted thoughts." Howroyd's success story is a living example of how specific strategies around preparedness and presentation allowed her to leverage both, and ultimately drive her to achieve an aggressive (by any measure) goal of magnitudinal success.

Howroyd, my mother, many of you, and I are all-in on the accolades and financial model of owning and operating our own businesses. These benefits are undeniable and, largely, the motivation for many of us. But let's be honest: while women are leaning into entrepreneurship at record-shattering rates, it is a long, hard journey to make it to the level of profile with which our visions begin. I would be remiss to misrepresent the hardships and challenging realities involved in launching, growing, and maintaining your own business venture.

My mother inherited her entrepreneurial spirit from her father, but my grandmother spent her entire life working, and was much more comfortable relying on the perceived security associated with a job working for other people. My mother's mother could not relate to this entrepreneurial spirit in her daughter, and tried to kill it (not due to malice, but to a lack of understanding and appreciation) at every turn. Even after years as a successful entrepreneur running beauty salons, my grandmother still wasn't a supporter. I've heard the story of when Mom decided to expand and take her business model to the next level by opening child care centers.

Initially, she faced financial struggles and needed a $2,000 loan from my grandmother. My grandmother's first response was to scold her daughter with the "told you sos" and doubt. Instead of offering the necessary support all business owners crave, my mother's mother coldly said, "You need to sit down somewhere and just go get a regular job like the rest of us. No one told you to be a big shot and open your own business!" My grandmother ultimately loaned her the money, but the conditions under which Mom had to receive it felt unfortunate. At a time when Mom desperately needed both financial and emotional support, she received negativity instead. As disheartening as this feedback was it's actually pretty common for those closest to us to inject doubt and negativity and become the biggest naysayers in our lives. As was the case with my grandmother, this negative reaction isn't rooted in evil intentions, but is based in a place of understandable fear; fear that their loved one will be disappointed, hurt, suffer hardships, and ultimately fail in their business pursuit.

Added to these universally shared fears are the historically haunting notions that many black Americans endure,
narratives similar to the ones Howroyd heard when she
first integrated into her Tarboro, NC high school. The
ignorant yet persistent narrative was that black Americans' purpose was tied to slave labor and therefore they
were only destined to serve others. My grandmother was a
daughter of the deep rural south and had never seen black
business owners. She had spent her entire life working for
other people, specifically cleaning houses, caring for children, and cooking for wealthy white people. For her, this
seemed to the be the fitting employment for black people.
So my mother's fierce determination to own and operate
her own business and be responsible for her own financial
destiny was not only out of the ordinary for my grandmother, it was downright scary! In a display of beautiful
irony, do you want to guess who was the first black person
my grandmother ever worked for? Her own daughter, my
mother. Once Mom's childcare facilities took off, she
needed help caring for the growing number of children
enrolled. My grandmother had over 30 years of experience caring for small children so my mother supplemented
that experience by sending my grandmother to community college for childcare education classes. Mom then
hired my grandmother as an employee and eventually my
grandmother became co-director of one of my mother's
locations. In the end the $2,000 loan that my grandmother
was so nervous about became a critical investment in her
own professional development and our family's legacy.

As beautifully as things turned out, Mom was hurt and
disappointed by my grandmother's initial skepticism and
criticism. Fortunately, my mother possesses the quality

that is most necessary for entrepreneurship (more than skill, vision, and experience combined) . . . grit.

Grit is the single most sought after quality when venture capitalists are looking for startup founders, as noted by Josh Linkner in his 2013 *Forbes* article. Grit is generally defined as taking personal responsibility instead of blaming others, maintaining clear goals and determination despite others' beliefs, and doubling down on self-confidence in the face of challenges. Challenges are inevitable when starting your own business, no matter how much intelligence, wealth, or professional connection you might have. And challenges will continue, even as you become well established and thrive. Because of that certainty, the ability to face those challenges head-on and rely on your grit factor is key for any successful business owner.

University of Pennsylvania researchers determined that grit was a better predictor of success than a person's IQ. While there are several factors associated with grit, it comes down to whether you have a "make it happen" attitude and are willing to do what it takes to grow your business in the face of financial setbacks, discrimination, other people's doubts or ridicule, and even your own periodic self-doubt. Grit is the ability to push through these types of challenges and trust that nothing worth having ever comes easy; furthermore, success and sacrifice tend to go hand in hand. Thank God my mother possesses a healthy amount of grit. That is why when met with my grandmother's (and many others') skepticism and criticism along the way, my mother forged ahead with her vision and still enjoys success in her businesses today.

Stories like my mother's reflect the hero status that many entrepreneurs enjoy in our society. We look at Mark

Zuckerberg, Steve Jobs, and even successful mom and pop small business owners as the best reflections of the great American dream. They were brave, took the risks many among us are not willing or capable of taking, and most importantly they made good on them. But there is another side of entrepreneurship. "The downside of being up" is how Jessica Bruder referred to it in her article, "The Psychological Price of Entrepreneurship."

Before they relish in success, many entrepreneurs struggle through bouts of despair, darkness, and sometimes debilitating anxiety. Business owners typically juggle many roles and face inevitable setbacks—declining profits, disputes with partners, fluctuating demand for your product, loss of customers, and often debt (both business and personal), or "going in the hole" along the way. Grit is defined as seeing the light at the end of the tunnel and working through those challenges, but at some point we must ask ourselves where is the line between being a gritty business hero and just being flat out irresponsible.

It is important for me to paint a full picture of what stepping out to start your own business can really look like. It would be irresponsible of me only to share the glorious highlights I've been blessed and privileged to enjoy along my journey. I simply cannot share my story of being a first generation college graduate, landing as an attorney at a prestigious law firm, then cultivating a second successful career as television and radio personality, without also sharing the dark moments of financial crisis, self-doubt, ridicule, anxiety, and despair I faced along the way.

When I began sharing with my friends, colleagues, and associates that I was leaving my successful law practice to move to Los Angeles to launch a career in media, they mostly thought I was joking or crazy. I was certainly not either. I had no connections and no real idea around exactly what I wanted to do in media, but I believed wholeheartedly in my ability to figure it out. I also found comfort in knowing that no one would take away my law license, so I could always come back to practice if things didn't work out. In that way it felt like I was playing with house money. But after making the move and narrowing down my focus to wanting a role as an on-air legal and political expert, I was completely invested in my goal. It no longer felt like house money because now it was real money tied to a real goal.

Throughout my four years in Los Angeles I went through a divorce, waited tables, performed hourly contract legal work to pay the bills, and simultaneously went on any television or radio show I could book (unpaid) in order to develop a reel. If I were ever going to move to the next level (and ever get paid), I needed the experience and the evidence of my on-air work to show my skill. While I was blessed to be invited to be a guest on anyone's show in the beginning, it was a real challenge because those appearances didn't pay any money but they required four or five hours of my day (researching the topic, commuting in LA traffic, doing hair and makeup to be camera ready . . . nobody likes a diva!). This meant long days, working at various law firms for nine hours a day doing contract work to pay for minimum living expenses on top of making these free on-air appearances daily.

The good news was that the momentum of my media appearances was building: I was growing my audience and producers wanted to use me more. All good! But while I was doing a great job of growing my on-air brand, the appearances ate away at the time I was available to work the practical jobs I still needed to survive. This dilemma was real and very challenging for me to navigate responsibly. On one hand I was no dummy and I knew I had rent, car payments, insurance, student loans, groceries, and a slew of other expenses that needed to be covered. On the other hand I didn't leave my flourishing law practice and move across the country to be a waitress or contract lawyer. I made that decision and chose that temporary sacrifice to chase my passion and dream of continuing my work as an advocate and voice for the voiceless on a larger platform. I sought to empower others and make the law and political engagement more accessible to all people by using my gifts of relatable communication, legal knowledge, and appealing aesthetic. I certainly wasn't going to get closer to that goal by turning down the hard-fought opportunities to be on-air building my media presence and participating in the national dialogue to go bill out at twenty-five dollars an hour doing contract work. I had a real conflict between what was the responsible or right thing to do. If I had to make the same choices today, I'm legitimately uncertain which I would choose.

I can tell you what ended up happening.

I doubled down on my television and radio appearances, worked all the hours I could when I wasn't on-air and prayed for God's will over my life. During the year that followed, great things happened and horrible things happened. The great things included appearing daily on networks including the NFL Network, CNN, HLN, TV One, Fox News, and Fox Business. I was even hired by HLN as a contributor and was making some money when I would appear, a great supplement to the money I was still earning as a contract lawyer. But it just wasn't enough to counter the deep debt I'd incurred the previous three years while trying to make it in media. Enter the horrible things: my cell phone was constantly being cut off due to nonpayment, which really was a problem because I relied on it heavily for media bookings. I would often have to stretch twenty-five dollars a week for my entire food budget. Gas was now for special occasions so I was commuting on public transportation two hours each way to get to my legal contract job. I didn't have money to pay for my yearly car inspection or registration so I kept getting tickets and even was towed once while I was inside a studio doing an appearance. I was also two months behind on my rent, and during my last week in LA I received a notice from my car lender saying that after three months without a payment they were finally repossessing my vehicle. I couldn't blame them. I was all out of chips.

A month before I received the car repossession notice, I'd taken my last $250 and opted to use it for a plane ticket to New York City instead of paying my car payment (I know, I know, but wait for it). I flew myself out there and couch surfed at my dear college friend's place while I took meetings with every network in town. Something needed to break and break quick. Weeks later after I returned to LA (repossession notice in hand) my cell phone rang (I'd smartly decided to pay that bill that month). It was my manager telling me that CBS News made an offer to hire me as a full-time network correspondent! They were launching their 24/7 digital streaming property and felt my radio and commentary experience was a perfect fit.

They also cited being impressed with my ability to debate Bill O'Reilly in the appearances they'd seen (those free segments finally paid off!). CBS News offered a handsome salary and covered my moving expenses because I was set to start the new role in NYC in three weeks. In that one phone call my life went from feeling like complete despair to ecstatic hope. I was thrilled. It was the opportunity of a lifetime and it was exactly on time. The biblical saying "He may not come when you want him, but he's always on time" never resonated with me more than it did in that moment.

To this day, I've never felt more grateful and relieved than when on the brink of eviction and repossession, I received that offer from CBS News. I learned many important lessons from that experience. But most important I learned the lesson of gratitude. Specifically, I learned not to wait until your darkest moment or your breaking point to exercise gratitude. Stay in a space of gratitude at all times and especially when things are challenging. I started to practice gratitude more intentionally once I moved to NYC. I write in a gratitude journal almost daily, a simple line expressing one thing I'm grateful for each and every day. The hard days typically have the best gratitude prayers. I also do something very deliberate for someone else when I'm having a particularly rough time.

While I'm still eternally grateful for my opportunity at CBS News, my experience there included lots of challenges. Having your first full-time job in news be at the Tiffany network doesn't come without many rough days and moments of self-doubt. On my roughest days I would be even more purposeful about being grateful, and finding a way to share that with others. The network had a cart full of free books (from the countless authors who pitched their works to the network). On the days marked with more challenge than I wanted to handle, I'd take as many books as I could carry and donate them to the nursing home down the street from my apartment in Harlem. It's the kind of thing I've always done but doing it with a certain urgency on my toughest days served the community but also served my spirit. It literally took the day's negative energy and gave it such a new positive purpose that I almost forgot what had me so upset before. I've been blessed always to have believed in myself and my vision, and to have a select few in my circle who give me unwavering support, but it is inevitable that on the way to success, challenges will come, and come hard.

From one entrepreneur's story of seemingly smooth-going, and almost immediate success to others' of steadfastness through challenge, at least one thing is true: Everything *does* matter! From the substance of our lives, our work, and the other diligent steps toward preparation, to the careful consideration of how we maintain our composure and present through it all, it takes all we have in our arsenals to fight our way to the full potential of our power.

CHAPTER 6

THE COURT OF PUBLIC OPINION

With Insight from Dr. Frank Luntz

"Women have the advantage in talking about the family, the neighborhood, and the community. They are at a disadvantage when it comes to communicating to the brain."

—DR. FRANK LUNTZ

When I call for tapping into one's pretty power, it is all about messaging: creating and controlling a particular narrative that permits you to convey a particular message about who you are, what you offer professionally, and how that maximizes your power ascent. Whether you're meeting with clients, presenting to partners at a firm, or serving on of a board of directors at a nonprofit, you are always sending a message with your presentation and communication, so it is all too important to be aware of what yours is and be intentional about it.

To this point, we've explored a few different aspects

of aesthetic packaging: style narrative, clothing choices, body image, hair and makeup . . . most of the things that come to mind immediately when asked to consider how you look and present. But there are other aspects of "pretty packaging" that can scream the wrong or unintended message to everyone with whom you interact. If you have no clue what I'm talking about, this chapter is a great little primer from a man who "reads" women's messages for a living.

Frank Luntz is a highly sought after public opinion guru. He specializes in political and communication consulting, has worked as a pollster, and appears frequently on Fox News, CBS News, and across other media and television outlets. Luntz is *the* guy to call when you want to figure out what people are thinking and why they are thinking it. He is called on to conduct focus groups all across the country to dissect attitudes, analyze emotions, and synthesize opinions. Very interesting stuff! His expertise and experience allow him to accurately measure and deliver research that explains what turns people off or makes them tune in. He is a messaging king.

Much of Luntz's work focuses on language and word choices. He coaches both men and women on delivering messages—political, business, or otherwise—but for our purposes and consideration of *Pretty Powerful*, I wanted to spend some time with him discussing what he's learned about his female clients. I wanted to know if he's found specifics about what shapes a woman's narrative or public opinion. In addition to all the other branding elements we typically think of, my conversation with Luntz provided some insight into how women can intentionally shape narratives around their professional selves by managing their mannerisms, word choice, body language, and even topics of conversation.

Luntz conducts an interesting exercise with the public where he'll have, say, a 40-year- old woman and a 60-year-old man stand up, and he will ask, "Which of these two has a better grasp of issues surrounding education?" Luntz says the woman will typically win favor four- or five-to-one, even sometimes as much as ten-to-one. He'll then ask, "Who do you trust more when it comes to national security and fighting terrorism?" And with this question, the man will be preferred by three- or four-to-one. Luntz uses the exercise to show that there are inherent biases that still exist between the genders, and we need to be aware of them. He's studied that woman have a distinct advantage over men in areas like healthcare and education, where there's a greater emotional component associated with the issue, and men will have an advantage over women in issues like national security, defense, and areas that are more numbers oriented. He does point out, however that societal changes and advancements have shifted how young people might respond. They function as if they don't really see gender in the same way. Luntz says, "Under age 30 it doesn't matter, but if you're over age 50 it still does. It still has an impact on how we think. And it creates both positive and negative biases. Women have the advantage in talking about the family, in talking about the neighborhood, and talking about the community. They have the advantage in telling a story and in communicating to the heart. They are at a disadvantage when it comes to communicating to the brain, and there's always exceptions to this. Margaret Thatcher [first female prime minister of Great Britain and controversial figurehead during her time in office] was thought to have no heart whatsoever. And same thing with Hillary Clinton, [and] to some degree with some other global leaders, Indira Gandhi. These women had the traits that we see in both women and men in terms of toughness, fortitude [plus] something emotional inside that most men don't have." Luntz shares one of his own biases that, "I'm actually more critical of men for being unable to articulate human appeal that women [have] than I am for women being unable to communicate the 'toughness.' [When women don't have that toughness], I don't see it as a disadvantage, I actually think women in a communication, in a political sense and in a business sense, have an advantage because they have the same type of knowledge and wisdom when it comes to more tangible aspects of business and politics, but they have something that men don't have, which is the ability to articulate that in a human approach rather than a cold clinical approach which is what most men do. [For that reason] I think an effective woman will do a better job than an effective man." Luntz gives the messaging advantage to women. He says our advantage is due to our ability to articulate a human appeal while also being substantively competent on the issues. Particularly when women talk about their family and community, it immediately makes people tune in and pay attention. Getting the audience's attention is an important first step in effectively delivering our desired substantive message. Men tend to have the competence but struggle to appeal emotionally. Our ability to do both at the same time creates a powerful professional advantage that we should never be afraid to use, and I really want to highlight this so that the women who are naturally doing this keep it up, and the ones who don't do it for fear of something (perhaps playing into a gender stereotype?), feel more comfortable embracing the more "human" side.

I asked Luntz for examples of words or body language or things that he sees women doing that effectively communicate the warmth and emotional strength he is talking about, specifically what he sees working.

Luntz explained, "A woman is more likely to touch her heart when she's talking about an emotional issue or something about family or community. She literally will touch her heart. And that physical gesture communicates authenticity in her communication. In terms of actual communication— words that they use—women are just more likely to say 'we' and 'us,' and men are more likely to say 'I' and 'me.' " The "we" mentality implies that a the person saying it has not just their own best interest in mind, but also the interest of all, and that typically resonates well with others.

I was curious about the impact of smiling. I asked Luntz if he had any observations around the incorporation of the smile, how women do that, how it is perceived as an attribute to the kind of more emotional aspect he was talking about. I wondered if there is such a thing as too much smiling, to the extent that it undermines authority and being taken seriously. Luntz thinks it is all based on the individual, but was definitive that radiating a positive energy is what's effective. He used a few politicians as examples.

He gave Kirsten Gillibrand, junior U.S. senator for New York as an example. He says she comes across as "one of the most positive [and] uplifting, she is the epitome of a sunrise. With rays of light just all around her and her whole communication, everything about her is one of positive energy." (It proves an incredible contrast to the senator whom Gillibrand replaced, Hillary Clinton.) Luntz then gives an opposing example of another senator, retired (whose name he doesn't want to say), "She would have liked to have radiated positive energy, but everything about her was exactly the opposite. So it really does depend on the individual you are speaking about." Luntz says it is the same thing in business, "There are some CEOs that just have that positive aura around them and there are others—and I'll say particularly out of Silicon Valley—some of the women have just a more negative demeanor to them. I can't characterize it because it really does depend on the individual."

I asked Luntz to tell us if he were coaching someone and she said, "I'm running for this office, or I'm going for this CEO position, and I've been getting feedback that I'm not coming across as having a positive energy, and I'm just not connecting," how would he coach her to get closer to that goal. I know she can't duplicate it, but getting closer to that Gillibrand or that warm fuzzy feeling that some of these women possess and that has been seen as a value add.

Luntz says, "It's storytelling, rather than facts. And it's storytelling that involves emotion rather than statistics. It's very hard not to be engaged, not to be interactive if you're explaining something about your family or your community. And it comes naturally to most women. That does not come naturally to most men. Men won't do that. Men feel like they're being weak. And the problem is what they're actually [coming across as] being is mean."

Specifically, he points to women's ability to be incredibly effective storytellers, therefore, framing our advice or positions in story format is one way (certainly not the only way) to effectively assert ourselves on topics not traditionally thought to be our stronghold. One could easily and justifiably critique the very dynamic that distinguishes between issues where men and women are thought to hold separate authority. But that does not change the fact that for many people (especially older people) those distinctions do exist on a conscious or subconscious level, so it is a great tool to be able to combat those presumptions.

Other than when a woman physically touches her heart, I asked Luntz what epitomizes or personifies what women do either thoughtfully, maybe even subconsciously, that radiates that connectedness in their physicality as they are speaking.

"Yes, so you've got Barbara Mikulski [senior U.S. senator from Maryland]," Luntz says, "who will always make fun of her height [she's stands at a powerful 4'11"]. And she's tough as nails, and yet you have a sense that's she's fighting for you, and you want to hug her because you believe that she'll hug you back. So here's someone who doesn't radiate that [standard] positive, she radiates a street brawler for the best reasons. Street brawler for you, fighting for the things that you need, and that's very different. Who else can I look at on the Senate side? Because I've actually looked at them and studied them. Oh, Carly Fiorina. She tells a joke, that people say to her you don't smile enough. It's not a joke, it's true. Voters thought she was either the smartest or second smartest candidate and they believe that she was totally qualified to do the job but they did not believe that she had a heart. And here's someone who had an amazing presentation, they wanted her because they thought she would slice and dice Hillary Clinton better than anyone and she'd get away with it. But when you ask what are the fears or what are the concerns that voters have, even among Republicans, they just felt that she had no emotion. So it hurt her in the end."

As for the hyper-scrutiny women in politics face, it is a bipartisan issue. Carly Fiorina was continuously reported on for her failure to smile enough. From CBS News, to the *Washington Post*, numerous media outlets dissected whether she should smile more. She poked fun at and called out the superficial criticism during a debate by answering the question of what her greatest weakness was by saying, "Gee, after the last debate I was told I didn't smile enough," then she beamed. It was awesome. She very effectively, yet subtly, reminded us all how she was being treated differently as the only woman on that stage.

Luntz stated, "Meg Whitman should not have lost California by as much as she did. Once again, here is someone with the most incredible résumé and success story [but she was] not as emotional as [her opponent] Jerry Brown. She lost in a landslide and a lot of that had to do with never bringing the human element into the conversation."

I asked Luntz to share what any woman in business or politics can do to consciously tap into bringing that human component into her presentation. Number one, Luntz says is to "talk about her kids, because that connects to everyone. It connects to women more than men, but it connects to everyone. [And] number two, talk about the future, not the past. Because the future is what we're focused on and we'll listen to it because we will feel that she is planning for the future which is something that guys don't always do." For those of us who don't have children, I'd imagine that talking about family could help to achieve some of the same effect.

In addition to *what* is being discussed, how it sounds when it's being said also sends a message. Hillary Clinton has constantly been criticized for her tonality of voice. When Luntz speaks to his women clients about their tonality, I asked him if there is a particular sweet spot he recommends to project good affective communication. Luntz says, "Don't yell. And if you're in a room, and there are a thousand people, and you're at a microphone, remember that the microphone projects you, don't feel like you have to shout into it. It doesn't come across well." No one likes to be yelled at, makes sense.

Clinton has much in the way of political baggage, policy positions, or other substantive issues to critique. Yet, she is continuously being assessed by her appearance and even the sound of her voice. A constant critique by the media, the public, and even highbrow political analysts has been Clinton's habit of speaking in a way that can sound like she's yelling. Headlines from mainstream newspapers, think pieces on Facebook and Twitter, and opposing candidates themselves have seared Clinton for "screaming, shouting, and yelling." There are textbooks that go through the sexist theories around women "yelling" and our general hysterical nature. There was even a time when "female hysteria" was considered a mental illness and viable defense in the court of law. The notion of female hysteria even reared its ugly head after the first Republican primary debate when Trump accused Megyn Kelly, journalist and former defense attorney, of having "blood coming out of her wherever."

Whether it is historical sexism or not, Luntz's research shows that women are certainly ineffective in communication when we are perceived to be yelling. His advice is simple: don't yell. Instead, let the microphone do the work for you. If you are in a room without a microphone do your best to project from your diaphragm and tap into the lower register of your voice, but fight the urge to force projection from your throat because that can undermine your vocal reach and it does not come across well.

While I knew perhaps it probably wasn't his expertise, I couldn't help but ask Luntz for his thoughts on physical presentation when sending his women clients into a situation where they're going to be observed publically. His response was priceless, but you can't blame me for trying while I had the attention of this man who studies women for a living: "Are you nuts? You're asking me about clothing?" I had to catch my breath from laughing before wrapping the conversation, but not before he named world-renowned economist Laura Tyson as near the top of his *personal* best-dressed list. He cited her ability to appear bright but not overbearing, professional, and perfectly enhancing her personality. He went on to say she was brilliant but also approachable, and her clothing and style choices accurately reflected those personal and professional dynamics. Another point proven. Everyone has an opinion, even if they acknowledge theirs as not being expert. When considering our pretty power, the entire picture is one that will be in question. Whether it's our look, the way we speak, the words we use, or even the volume at which those words are being said, it is a miss if each of these elements is not maximized to its full potential.

CHAPTER 7

TRIAL BY FIRE

With Insight from Marcia Clark

"Some of this is biological . . . women are the standard bearers of beauty, so to speak. That doesn't mean we shouldn't try to rise above it though."

—MARCIA CLARK

"The Trial of the Century" stuck out like a sore thumb to me. I had such a preliminary interest in this juxtaposition and intersection of law and media, and that's probably why I chose the career path I'm currently on. I shared with Marcia Clark that after school I would watch every moment of the trial at the hair salon my mother owned at the time, to which Clark replied without skipping a beat, "She could have helped me then." This woman is kind of amazing!

The first thing I needed to do when I spoke to Marcia Clark for the first time was express gratitude. Acknowledging her as the first female attorney I ever saw in a courtroom (who wasn't on a TV show or in a movie) was an important part of my ability to see myself trying cases one day. Representation is important. As Clark says, "If you can't see it, you can't be it." For some people they find examples of their aspirations within their own homes and families. That's a huge blessing. For some of us, we have to find those examples in the greater community or the media. Seeing Clark in that courtroom was powerful because she wasn't just in the room, she was a leader in the room. She was crashing the boy's club party.

Becoming a lawyer was a super long-shot dream of mine. I do not come from a family of college educated people. Seeing Clark—a woman—practicing law in a courtroom was pretty huge for me. It changed me. I am from the South, and growing up I did not see women in the role of a lawyer.

Clark shares that it always makes her so happy to hear that seeing that awful debacle was actually inspiring in a good way, and that something good came of it. That "debacle," of course, was the 1994 O. J. Simpson (former National Football League star and actor) murder case and criminal trial held at the Los Angeles County Superior Court. Simpson was tried (and acquitted) on two counts of murder for the deaths of his ex-wife Nicole Brown Simpson, and her friend Ron Goldman. The trial lasted just under a year, and the case has been described as the most publicized criminal trial in American history.

It was very powerful for many of us. Many women are out-graduating men in law school or are at least on track with them. That was not always the case. I do think women like Clark are very much responsible for that shift in trend. I thank Clark for that.

Clark was the only woman in a special prosecution unit in the Los Angeles District Attorney's office called the "Special Trials Unit." Clark recalls, "There were instances of sexism. Not necessarily the men who were in the unit with me but in management. The boss of the unit certainly was at that time. I got second class treatment by him, but there were only four men in the unit."

The men who were actually in the trial courts did not give Clark a hard time. She said, "It was really interesting who does and who doesn't. You would think that police in general would be the hardest sell because that was *the* most male dominated—particularly homicide—and yet interestingly (although initially they'd [express], 'Oh, God, a girl's handling my case,') they were cool. It was like, 'Okay, you're going to work hard, okay, that's fine.'"

I was curious to know, when Clark was assigned the "Trial of the Century" what the politics were like. I imagined there would be jealousy as surely every prosecutor would want that case. I asked Clark how it felt to be assigned that case. At the time, Clark did not know how big O. J. Simpson was, so it was not as big a deal as one would think. Simpson had not really been in the public eye that much, she laughed, "I mean, I know it's hard to imagine at this point."

I kind of remembered that. I was a kid, but I didn't really know who he was in the same way you would know who some of the other more famous athletes-turned-actors were until the charges were in play. Clark continued, "For many of us, it was that way. Even those who knew about his football career had not heard from him in a really long time. So it wasn't clear to me that it [would be] our Special Trials Unit, [which] was devoted to handling high-profile cases. The fact that a celebrity was involved in the case was not itself a big deal. That's what we do. It's what we handle." Of course. It's Los Angeles. Clark explained, "Whether it's high profile because it's a night stalker or it's high profile because a celebrity is on one side or the other, it was just what we did. So to say that there was widespread jealousy or a big political push from a lot of the others, no, there wasn't. There were only five or six of us in the Special Trials Unit at the time. I had handled a domestic violence murder just recently. I had handled DNA cases prior to that, so my particular experience was relevant to this." Clark was an obvious choice. Her bosses felt, "She's the right one for this. Give her the case." It really wasn't a big deal.

As serious and titillating as the actual details of the case being tried were, everyone remembers when the case turned into, "What is Marcia Clark wearing to court?" I remember the headlines. I was about twelve years old. I remember asking, "Why isn't anyone asking about Johnny Cochran's hair?" As a member of the black community, we knew Cochran from representing Michael Jackson ("The King of Pop") and some high profile police brutality cases. Everyone knew Cochran was flashy. Cochran liked his silk ties and silk suits. That was his thing. I wondered, "Why are we so obsessed with how Marcia Clark is wearing her hair, and what color her suit is? And how short it is or how not short the skirt is? And not paying that same attention to the others in the courtroom?"

On top of preparing for openings and order of

examining witnesses, Clark now had to think about this. I asked her when the appearance part and the more overt sexism aspect started taking shape. Clark shares, "It happened way before we started calling witnesses. It happened early, early on. It was when we started going to court. It felt like it started happening after the preliminary hearing, after we started going to court for pretrial motions. That's when it felt like I started hearing stories about stuff like this. To be honest, I didn't take it seriously. The media is so goofy, of course they are. I had a long history of avoiding the press whenever possible. I don't care if a case is high profile to the press. I care what the jury thinks."

Clark was not trying to be a reality star. And there was no such thing back then. Clark said, "I really ignored it, laughed at it, thought it was just silly. It just wasn't a focus." There was never a point where Clark felt people were taking it seriously or that it was having any impact at all on the jury. She said, "I've got to tell you, my fears about the jury were completely separate from that. I never got the sense that they gave any credence to my appearance. I never got the sense that they cared at all what my hair, or makeup or clothes looked like." She laughs, "I really didn't."

It became very clear to Clark before the actual trial started—somewhere in the pre-trial motion stages—that everybody else on the outside was caring, and that the focus turned into gavel-to-gavel coverage on television all day long. It was the origin of Court TV. I wouldn't have a career doing what I'm currently doing, but for this case. This was the spawn of the on-air legal analyst career path. It did not exist before this case. It was the genesis of it all.

Some call it "evil-genius," depending on who is doing the coverage.

I've had the pleasure of working with Greta Van Susteren, Nancy Grace, Vinnie Politan, and some other originators of this craft, and we do talk about what we're going to wear. We absolutely consider what our wardrobe choices translate in terms of messaging. For my weekly O'Reilly segment, if I'm going to talk about abortion or rape or something that's really, really heavy, I find myself deciding very intentionally to wear a white dress or pearls or something soft because I know that I'm going to have to make a hell of a gritty argument that has intense content. Clark reacted, "You're smart to do it because I don't think there's any escape for women. I really don't. Because some of this is biological, I think. Women are the standard bearers of beauty so to speak and I think it is partly the animal in us. That doesn't mean we shouldn't try to rise above it though. The fact that we're kind of hard-wired for it though, but we also have free will. We also have intelligence." Clark laughs, "We're not animals." She keenly points out that women are the historical standard bearers of beauty and our appearance is tied to our biological purpose. But Clark is also quick to point out that these truths don't mean we shouldn't try to rise above it.

Clark continued, "We can make a choice to change the focus and not constantly pan a woman for her appearance—her hair, makeup, clothes—and say, 'You know what, can we go ahead and focus, let's elevate ourselves a little bit and look at and listen to what she has to say?' I think we can make that choice even though we are kind of hard-wired to notice a woman's looks, but let's not pander to it. It's one thing when you're talking about a model. Somebody who is putting themselves out there on a physical level. Okay, that's what you're doing, then the men should be judged that way too. There's a superficiality to the way women are judged on their looks that is more unfair."

I agree we should absolutely continue to push for continued growth and change in the way women are viewed as complete, intelligent, capable beings regardless of what we look like. But obviously, we are not there yet as a society, and in the meantime I want every woman to receive every opportunity she's worked for and if being more astute to the appearance-based dynamic can assist in her power ascent, I'm a strong advocate for it.

Clark and I seemingly disagree on this point, because she feels that women who pay too much attention to their looks are pandering. That's certainly an understandable point of view, and I'm sure many women feel the same. I happen to believe that if this pretty power consciousness will get people to hear what women have to say in a quicker, more effective way, the pandering is worth it.

Looking back, Clark does not have any regrets about focusing on the case rather than on her aesthetic and would do it all the same again. She explains, "Let me put it this way, if I started becoming glammed up and let all the makeup people who started crowding the courtroom quarters start putting makeup, doing my hair, doing my makeup I would have been slammed for that. Then I become a party doll. 'Oh, yeah, look at the new glammed up Clark.'

"And they did it to me anyway—even though there was no makeover for my hair. My perm grew out. It looked more scraggly than usual. I didn't have time or money to go and get it re-permed, so I had to blow it out because my hair is naturally straight. I had to blow it out, and they called that 'my makeover.' Okay, so look how crazy that went. Can you imagine, can you imagine, if I really had a makeover? Holy Mother of God! My 'makeover' consisted of a friend who loaned me a concealer pencil that my son promptly stuck in a sprinkler pipe drain because it fit. You know, he thought it was cute. Yeah, and so, there was my makeover and look what happened."

The media took it and ran with it. Clark said, "Is there any way to win this? No, there's no way to win this. Either you are too glammed-up and not taken seriously or they think I look like a ragbag because my suits are off the rack—by the way, at the time, I had no idea what they were even talking about." Clark laughs, "Where else do you buy your suits?"

So how do we win this? Clark says, "You don't win that battle. And the other part of it is, 'Oh, you should have been softer.' Really? I should have been softer and then what are you going to say? Oh, I'm a cream puff and I can't handle it? Why don't they bring a man in to handle it? Because obviously, I'm just a little girl." Clark feels that for her to try to combat the media machine and everything else at play at that time would have been a fool's errand. If she attempted to "soften" her appearance she would have come across as a lightweight litigator not equipped to deal with the seriousness in front of her. If she tried to look "tough" she would have been labeled the hyper-aggressive bitch.

She reflected on that. "It's one thing when you're addressing the camera as a commentator and these are short little spots that we have a couple minutes here, a couple minutes there, or even seconds, that's one thing, that you can smile for the camera and kind of sugar coat while you stick the knife between the shoulder blades. But when you're on camera hours and hours and you're in front of a judge arguing motions or in front of a jury arguing the case you really can't play those kind of media games and smile. You have to be who you are. For prosecutors, especially in front of a jury that is not a welcoming jury, the very last thing you want to do is present some kind of fire and brimstone arguments, or anything kind of razzle-dazzle. What you want to do is be the one who is objective and fair and neutral and, you know, look, 'I'm just presenting the truth, I have no personal agenda here.' You have to appeal to the jury, and that means you have to adjust how you are presenting. But you do it for the jury, you don't do it for the public."

Clark had to look at who she had in the jury box and think carefully about what this jury was going to accept, and what this jury was going to reject out of hand. Clark would adjust herself accordingly. She says, "It's different when I'm on camera talking and commenting on cases. That's a whole different thing."

When Clark was going in front of twelve in a box, her prescription to convey objectivity and authority suggests, "Know. Your. Audience. For example, I'm going into the courtroom. It's really great that you want to pound the podium and say, 'He deserves the death penalty, and he deserves blah, blah, blah.' That's cool. You want to do that, but what does your jury want? What will your jury accept? What will your jury hear? You have a timeframe. Sometimes the message you're delivering is not one they are going to accept no matter what you do, but do your best. If you're facing a hostile jury, don't think you're going to take off your shoe and pound the podium. You're going to turn them off more. They're going to hate you even more. So you want to be as reasonable, as calm, as rational, and logical as you possibly can and hope to appeal to whoever on the jury is willing to look past whatever the reasons are for resistance. And the reasons could be myriad. For example, Casey Anthony. She's a sweet young thing, and we don't believe she would kill her baby. And we don't like the dad. You have to gauge what is what, where the popularity is in your case. Because there always is an element of popularity, one side or another, then deal with that accordingly."

Clark shared another example in Los Angeles of the Phil Spector trial. She recalls the story, "He was a music producer, very famous, crazy, nuts. Not only nuts, but they put a parade of women to say, 'He drew a gun on me too.' He was that kind of crazy. For a defendant like that? You can definitely stand up and pound the podium, and talk about the evil intent and the fact that he was a time bomb waiting to happen. That he finally exploded. No big surprise. He did a woman in with a gun as he's been torturing women his whole life. That's great. And that jury will accept that, because that's who your defendant is. When you have a Casey Anthony or on the complete other side of it, someone like O. J. Simpson who is beloved and is very popular and who has this wonderful kind of affable demeanor on camera, you can't do that. You better watch. So you always have to gauge your audience. I would say that's true in the boardroom as well. Think about who you're presenting to. Now that doesn't mean you have to wear different clothes. In fact, my advice would be to wear clothes that are the least obtrusive, the least eye-catching that you possibly can, because you want to play-up your message and downplay your appearance. That doesn't mean look bad. It just means, no cleavage. Don't distract."

Clark tried the O. J. Simpson case in front of the cameras over twenty years ago, before the age of Instagram, viral videos, and reality TV. I asked Clark if she tried the case today, would she think about the aesthetic component more and how she would approach that piece of it. Clark is not sure that she would change anything. She explains, "I'm not sure. In fact, I'd want to downplay my appearance even more, because with so much opportunity to take the photographs and share them around the world, what I'd probably wish I could do is wear a moo-moo. And I'd like to wear the same thing every day. But what I'd want to do is actually make it as little of an issue as possible and try and dial that out of it as much as I could. It's hard. It's very hard. But I'd want to probably be very careful about what I said and wore outside the courtroom in terms of knowing that everything is going to be captured on camera. The minute I walk out of the courtroom, of course in the courtroom as well, everything is going to be shared. I can't imagine the daunting experience of a case as heavily covered as that one was, with all of these outlets. It boggles my mind."

Just think about the social media memes. The memes from an O. J. Simpson's murder trial would've been insane. Clark agreed, "Yes, craziness. And that's why I think in today's world, judges must be very, very careful what they do in terms of allowing media access. I'm in favor of cameras in the courtroom. I am. But I do think there has to be limitations. When the jury's out, the cameras must be out, because otherwise, what's the point of having hearings outside the presence of the jury?"

Fortunately every powerful woman isn't under the relentless microscope of 24/7 television coverage as they embark on the serious work they pursue. But Clark's experience isn't completely removed from that of women all across our country in boardrooms, trading floors, and courtrooms absent media coverage. With Instagram, Facebook, and Twitter everyone is a journalist and they're all telling a story that you're subject to being a part of.

The media's treatment of Clark was not wonderful, but it was actually the least of her issues. Her biggest issue was the judge because the jury takes its cue from the judge. If the judge is treating her like a second-class citizen—which Judge Ito did—the jury is going to do it too. Clark recalled, "It did not matter what went on in court. He was twice as hard on me, demeaning to me, condescending to me, and this went on daily. And that was the most disheartening thing. And what can I do about that? If I call him on it, it's worse. So when Tammy Bruce [radio talk show host and progressive feminist, then president of the LA chapter of the National Organization for Women] came forward to him and spoke to him, I didn't know it. She didn't come to me first. She did it on her own."

Bruce compiled a tape of all the instances of Ito showing sexist disrespect to Clark in the courtroom and went to him and someone else and said, "You're treating her unfairly and it's very obvious that you are treating her much more harshly than the men. You're really demeaning to her. We believe she can take care of herself, but what you're sending is a message to the jury that they should treat her that way so you need to stop it. This affects justice." Judge Lance Ito would instruct the jurors not to be distracted by the hemline of Clark's skirts in the courtroom and while the male attorneys were referred to as Mr. Cochran or Mr. Bailey, she was simply Marcia. It was a blatant undermining of Clark's authority in the courtroom day after day.

Clark recalls, "He didn't believe them. He didn't believe them. And that's why they put together the video clips. When they did that, and again, I didn't know this was happening until after the fact, but when they did that, for a period, he actually went, 'Oh, my God! I can see it.' Or at least he said he did. For a period of about two to three weeks, I got to experience what it was like to be a man in that courtroom because he treated me with a little bit of respect. I actually got the respect that they did and suddenly I wasn't just Marcia, I was Ms. Clark. I was respected and there was just a better attitude. It didn't last, because he went right back to same old, same old. But for a little while there, I thought, 'Wow! That's what they get every day.' "

After the trial ended, I shared with Clark that I was amazed that Judge Ito shopped a judge show. Clark let us in on a little secret that the FX series (*The People v. O. J. Simpson: American Crime Story*) does not show to what degree Judge Ito was interested in the spotlight. "One hundred percent of the day, every day, he had celebrities running in and out of his chambers. Every. Single. Day. Holding court in chambers with all of these celebrities. Then they'd want to meet us, and he'd demand that we come into chambers to meet with these celebrities. It was horrifying. Horrifying."

Clark's experience (at least the one so documented and scrutinized) was one in which she expertly exerted her authority every day and even called out Judge Ito as he displayed blatant sexism during the course of the trial. As lead prosecutor she was running the show for the state, and it was incredible to watch her as the only woman at those lead counsel tables handle her business. Her presence gave me and countless other young girls and women permission to envision ourselves walking in her shoes.

Feminist theory would critique my argument around using your aesthetic to assist in your power ascent as indistinguishable from sexism. I submit that they are very distinguishable. Feminism isn't about there being a singular way to "be a woman." The entire point of the feminist movement was to ensure that a woman had a full scope of choice surrounding her ability to exist in this world. Part of that choice includes the ability to choose to turn an existing gender dynamic into an opportunity to advance her professional agenda.

Men and women absolutely care a great deal about what women look like. This is not necessarily rooted in romantic attraction. That's why both genders are at play when it comes to the ability to impact your professional impression with how you present physically. Women come to conclusions about one another based on what we look like all the time. Men, gay or straight, single or partnered/married, also assess women largely on what they look like before they know any additional information. Men are also absolutely assessed on what they look like. But women typically bring more to the table that can be assessed—wider fashion options, cosmetics, and more variety of hairstyles—and there is generally greater interest in how we present physically. Since there is such natural interest in how we look (as much as we may protest), this is certainly the existing climate so why not take full advantage as a way to control the narrative.

Controlling the narrative is something Clark was never afforded an opportunity to do. Before a single witness was called Clark remembers starting to hear the stories about her hairstyles and suit colors. While Clark made an effort to avoid the press and didn't take the initial buzz very seriously, the rest of the world had started to take serious notice of the female lead prosecutor of the case of the century.

Clark had no desire to be a part of the narrative. The only thing that mattered to her was meeting her burden of proof and obtaining justice for the families of Nicole Brown Simpson and Ronald Goldman. She was concerned with the jury and their opinion of her. When it came to others' judgmental and negative comments about her permed hair, the length of her skirts, and the color of her suits, Clark understandably felt the conversations were silly and beneath her and the important work she was doing. She ignored it, laughed at it, and thought it was all completely silly, but there can be a situation where the narrative can spin out of control regardless of what you do or don't do to be intentional about your appearance. During the O. J. Simpson trial Clark found herself being in a lose/lose situation. The devastating experience Clark endured around this issue was even depicted in the sixth episode of "*The People v. O. J. Simpson: American Crime*

Story" entitled "Marcia, Marcia, Marcia." When Clark's perm grew out, there were newspaper and television news headlines reading, "Marcia Clark Gets Makeover." There was no way she was winning this battle and the narrative around her was out of her control.

Her failure to be proactive about her look could have been a missed opportunity to influence that all-important jury. Clark still doesn't give the notion serious consideration, but sometimes people are not even aware of how much a person's appearance could influence their perception of that person consciously or subconsciously. We may never know, but it's worth considering that before she opened her mouth, the jury had made certain conclusions about Clark's preparation, credibility, and had a general sense of what kind of woman she was based on the way she looked. To the extent people start a narrative about you and what kind of person you are based solely on what you look like, I submit that you should be an active player in the narrative they create by deliberately messaging particular attributes by customizing your look.

I can comfortably admit that what Clark went through when she tried O. J. Simpson for double homicide in 1995 was both a critical assessment of her looks, and also a blatant sexist attack. At every turn she was undermined, discredited, and even demoralized at least in part because she is a woman. Whether you choose to lean into the pretty power grab or not, the treatment endured by Clark is completely unacceptable and no woman should have to deal with that.

Much of what I'm arguing in this book is based on the premise that women always have been and always will be assessed on how they look and present visually. I'm not suggesting that this dynamic is right, fair, or just. Only that it's not going anywhere for the foreseeable future, and so women could do themselves a tremendous favor by being keenly aware of the dynamic and making every effort to craft the message and impact to best position themselves for maximum professional gain.

CHAPTER 8

FACE VALUE

With Insight from Kirsten Haglund

"And because everyone has something different to offer, you can be the most beautiful person in the world, and if you're not confident in accepting inside yourself, you're not going to appear as the most beautiful person in the world to the people around you."

—KIRSTEN HAGLUND

At the age of twenty-eight, Kirsten Haglund has already accomplished much as a public speaker, online news anchor, and president of her foundation. Her personality and drive made her an expected success, but that success was catapulted after being crowned Miss America 2008.

The most important thing any Miss America does is travel the country promoting her platform, and Haglund's was deeply personal. She was a recovering anorexic.

Much of what I advocate in *Pretty Powerful* is about

being thoughtful, deliberate, and intentional when cultivating your appearance and overall presentation. But, let me be clear that this is not advocacy around holding yourself to an impossible physical ideal of perfection. "Perfection is the enemy of profitability" is a quote attributed to many prominent business leaders. Perfection is a distraction from the very necessary growth process that affords us all the opportunity to continue in our power ascent. Everything I am arguing is for the purpose of maximizing your professional trajectory. Anything (including a focus on perfecting your body, skin, voice, wardrobe, body language, or hair) that takes you off your ascent path is a detriment and should be reflected upon and seriously worked to overcome. Society, media, and our peer groups put enormous pressure on us to live up to impossible standards of perfection. To say it all sucks is putting it lightly, and entirely misses the point. In striving toward maximizing and leveraging our pretty power, I am not suggesting that women chase the impossible standards of others. I am suggesting that each woman give herself permission to decide for herself what her appearance ideal is based on her own professional goals and desires and leverage that. Haglund's dangerous path to her idea of perfection is a story worth sharing, and one that proves even the hardest challenges are possible to overcome, and turnaround into a success story.

Haglund was twelve years old when she started struggling with anorexia. She practiced classical ballet from the time she was three years old. She felt her whole identity was ballet. She so badly wanted and strived toward what is seen as the ideal ballet body type. That drive was coupled with the fact that everything else in her life at that time felt so out of control—her mom was diagnosed with breast cancer, and her older brother had started struggling with OCD (hand washing and door locking). Haglund recalls, "My pretty perfect little family world was just kind of spiraling. I felt like if I could just be the best ballet dancer that I could possibly be, then something in my life would make sense." Haglund felt ballet was something over which she could have some control. She explained, "And I had something. I had something to work toward, and of course that meant being thin. I was never fat. I mean, my mom is five feet eleven, and was always a string bean. Genetically, in our family, we're lean, but I super hyper-focused on that. I needed to look that way, be that way, and I associated that with goodness. So, it wasn't just about being thin, it was about being perfect. It was about being good. It was about being 'better than,' not being mediocre. Being exceptional. So it was a deep psychological, emotional, spiritual battle."

After three years, from age twelve to fifteen, Haglund said she became a shell of a person both physically and mentally. She was depressed and anxious, and shares that, "Some of my friends knew, but I really didn't tell a lot of people. I mean, you're a teenager, so it's the hardest time in your life anyway. Not to mention, being the crazy girl who has a problem. So I wasn't very open about it, and never really planned on being that open about it." And by the end of that confusing time in her life, she had no friends.

Her family suspected something was going on. But Haglund says, "No family likes to really talk about those things. Now my family is so open. We talk about everything which is so awesome. We make fun of each other.

It's great. But no, my parents didn't really want to talk about it. They thought I was supposed to be thin because I was a ballet dancer. But a couple of counselors at school would call home, and my mom would [say], 'Oh, no, she's just a ballet dancer. She just grew really fast, and blah blah blah.' But then, finally it got so bad, that my dad actually Googled the symptoms of an eating disorder and printed [it] off and [told my mom] I think your daughter has this. And that's when they got me into treatment."

With the support of doctors and nutritionists over a two-year period, Haglund was able to recover from her eating disorder and develop and maintain a body image that makes her feel confident and healthy. Haglund's story is one that is steeped in self-discovery, overcoming personal struggle, and selflessly championing for other women. That is the message that she tirelessly delivered throughout the country during her year as Miss America and still today. That is what *Pretty Powerful* is about.

Haglund said something to me that was so profound and powerful: when her eating disorder started, it was very much about not being mediocre, being exceptional, and being able to control her physical body image in that way was an avenue to express that exceptionalism. One of the things I am exploring it this book is just that. For better or worse, women are assessed on our looks, I would say even first. Haglund agreed, "Yeah. Not going away. It's not going away, it's been that way for centuries."

I still assert that women should use our "look" in a smart, resourceful way to advance us, but Haglund's experience illustrates such a slippery slope and how some people could go from being empowered by the awareness or use of their aesthetic and how to leverage it, to being obsessive or overly concerned with unrealistic expectations of perfection. It can go very wrong. But in true power play form, Haglund ultimately turned it into an opportunity.

Haglund tells the story of how she bravely went public with her struggle. "It kind of just happened. [In 2006] I was Miss Oakland County. I was speaking at a local Rotary Club businessmen's luncheon. And I had ten minutes to talk to the organization. They gave scholarships and they were sponsors, and I told them, thank you for investing in these young women's lives. And when the point came to talk about my platform and tell them what it is, I just blurted out, 'and I chose this because I struggled with an eating disorder.' I think I had just been talking and on a roll and it just came out. And my local director didn't even know. Then all of a sudden, obviously my face gets very red, and I start sweating and feeling so nervous, and [thinking] they're going to judge me. And I'm thinking, how stupid was I to just bring this up in a room full of suits, you know? They're not going to be compassionate or get it at all. But that really taught me something. Because after that, multiple men came up to me afterward, and there were some women, and they of course said, 'Thank you so much.' Multiple men came up and said things like, 'Thank you so much. I've been AA for twelve years, and it's so nice to hear someone be candid and open about their struggles.' Obviously not the same struggles, but similar, or, 'My wife had an eating disorder and my daughter is twelve years old, and I had no idea that these were such big issues.' I saw people open up. And you see the power of vulnerability. And I'm really glad I learned that lesson. That's what really motivated that desire to do even more. And obviously the job of Miss America gives you the opportunity to speak to exactly that target audience. Again, girls are feeling so insecure and so confused about their bodies, and their identity, and who they are, and what's their worth, and all that. They're looking up to me, and I can talk to them immediately about the issues. So after that I was sold."

It is a real opportunity that participating in pageants (an activity very much associated with leveraging a woman's physical attributes) afforded her a platform, and some could even say it was ironic that Haglund came out of her illness (developed during her youth as a ballet dancer) only to enter into pageantry, an environment that can easily breed reliance on the physical.

Her journey was a Cinderella story, if there ever was one. She won every single competition on her first try, complete with her first win in a fifteen dollar dress from the Salvation Army. But as she climbed the organization's "ladder" toward the ultimate success in the pageant system—earning the title and role of Miss America— she received a wake-up call around the level of thought, effort, and preparation needed to convey the specific essence of what being Miss America meant and represented.

She did not grow up doing pageants. She was not a toddler with a tiara. Haglund was seventeen and graduating from high school, and wanted a way to get some extra scholarships for college. She had known other women who had competed in the Miss America organization who had won a pretty significant amount of scholarship money from competing year after year after year. So she thought, "Well, I'll just enter my local pageant in Oakland County, Michigan, where I grew up. I thought

I'll wear my prom dress as my evening gown—which is what I did—and I sang an aria that I was working on with my voice teacher in high school, and wore a dress that my mom and I got at Salvation Army for literally fifteen dollars as my talent costume, so I really didn't put that much effort into it and ended up winning that local."

Haglund then left to start college. During her freshman year at college, on the weekends she returned home to do Miss Oakland County appearances, where she grew into that role little by little. When she went to compete at the Miss Michigan Pageant—the next level—representing her county, she didn't expect to win at all, "And I did, and then . . . fast forward six months to Miss America. I also did not expect to win."

Haglund won every single pageant she competed in during her first year. Wow! It was really quite a feat for her. She won $65,000 in scholarships . . . not bad for an "amateur"!

When Haglund won the local crown, she did not really think too much about putting on that fifteen dollar dress. Looking back, she says she observed the other local title holders, how they looked, and what they wore. At that time, no one had talked to her about her look and how she needed to present aesthetically when she made her appearances, or anything like that. But she was absolutely judged based on the package. To compete in her local pageant she had to go into the interview room and be interviewed in front of seven judges. She had never worn a suit before in her life. She had never worn pantyhose. She noticed that's what everyone else was wearing, so she followed suit (pun intended). Her suit coat had shoulder pads which made her feel extremely awkward. She said, "I was seventeen years old, so this was just a totally different world for me, but then when I became Miss Michigan, and then when I was competing for Miss America, then obviously there came a whole treasure trove of people telling you the look you should have."

Before she went to Miss America, she competed in a reality show with other state contestants who flew out to Los Angeles to live in a house together. They had professional stylists, fashion people, makeup artists, and hair stylists come in to give each of them a makeover of what they needed to change; what they needed to do to look more modern, young, and fashionable. As a seventeen-year-old local title winner and an eighteen-year-old Miss Michigan, Haglund had a little bit of a baby face, and was much younger than many of the other contestants. And most of the girls competing were in their early twenties, so Haglund stood out in that way. She had some people who were trying to make her look older by dressing her up in more mature suits and clothes to make her come across as more "substantial," more established, and more ready to handle the job. And then once they shot the reality show, they decided the "older" look was not what they wanted for any of the girls. "You all look way too old. You need to look your age." So they dressed them all down. No teasing the hair. Less makeup. More natural, and more fashion-forward clothing rather than very conservative suits and pantyhose. Haglund felt like it was mixed messaging. It was amazing how seriously the organization was taking their image, and the girls' images as a reflection of it.

Haglund shared that she saw the mixed messages and ultimately thought, "Because I didn't have a lot of skin in the game (thinking I didn't actually think I was going to win), [I thought], I'll just be myself. So I toned down the makeup. I did more of my own shopping and wore clothes that I thought were more what a normal eighteen-year-old girl would wear. But not looking like stripper or going out to party, you know, on a Friday night." Of course, we never want that. Haglund agrees, "Never. I think that was a good thing, and also because there's that tension between what you present on the outside and who you are on the inside. People have always told me that I'm an old soul, that I am very mature for my age, and that's why I did win at a young age. So even though I looked young and dressed for my age, and continued to dress my age on the road, you know, wearing jeans and casual things, as well, it was my heart and my smarts [that brought me success]. My brain showed them that I was ready for the job, rather than what I looked like on the outside."

Winning Miss America is very much about doing the job of Miss America. The nearly one hundred year old organization takes it very seriously. It is a true job with a salary with a full year-long commitment where Miss America travels 20,000 miles a month. Haglund became the face and brand of Miss America at nineteen years old, essentially a teenager, but now she needed to look like she's doing the job of a woman, able to do everything from speaking to legislators in Washington, DC, to being a spokesperson for various mission-driven organizations, doing public service announcements, commercials, or media interviews. As Miss America, you also serve as a spokesperson for sponsors, giving keynote speeches at conferences, business meetings, and community forums. Haglund recalls, "I mean, you're all over the place. And then doing things like signing autographs in a Walmart in the middle of Alabama."

Upon winning Miss America, Haglund first visited New York City to meet with several different designers who gave her lots of different clothes, everything from gowns to suits, to more casual wear. But she quickly realized, that the year she became Miss America the organization was really going through a transition in its board and leadership, and the vision of what Miss America was going to be. It was transitioning from this nineties and early two thousands where Miss America is always in a suit and never wearing the crown, to Miss America as more of an icon and a celebrity. Haglund had to decide what would work for her, while still representing the brand that was expected. She chose not to wear as many suits because she wanted to be a young, modern Miss America. She wasn't twenty-six or twenty-seven years old, and out of college. She was a nineteen-year-old girl, and she wouldn't feel comfortable and confident in doing the job if she didn't feel comfortable and confident in her wardrobe choices and the way she portrayed herself. Haglund said, "I stayed true to that and embraced a lot of the younger designers and younger looking clothes during the year. I remember at an event in Washington, DC, there was a woman who went to Miss America every year for this particular event, and it was an event for Jobs for America's Graduates, JAG, which is a great organization. It was in November or December, so I wore a red sweater dress and a pair of black tights with this pretty floral design, and black heels and my crown. So I looked very chic, festive. But we got complaints. To bring Miss America in every year, that I wasn't wearing a suit and tan pantyhose, that I didn't look how Miss America should look. And multiple people came to me during my year—also during my year I cut my hair. It was super long, and I said to the organization, 'I want to cut my hair,'—that was when that pixie bob was in. So I did, and a ton of people really loved it, but I had mostly men come up and look at my autograph picture, which for a while still had my long hair while I was changing it over, and would toss it back to me, and say, 'You looked way better with long hair.' I would have, literally, men look at me up and down and say, 'Oh, *you're* Miss America?' like they expected this sexpot. So it was really important to me to maintain my own personal style throughout the year, as well as, but yeah, you definitely feel pressure because everyone is looking at you. But besides the professional relationships that I was maintaining as a part of the organization, I mostly wanted to be a role model for young girls. And I wanted them to see someone who was confident in who she was, and not only taking the role seriously, but also expressing myself fashion-wise, and who I felt [I was]."

As Haglund focused on the overall goal, she first had to identify what she was specifically trying to represent and how that correlated to her accurately portraying the organization's ideals. This is a key lesson for each and every woman when they are pursuing a professional goal. Sure, when your goal is literally being the face of the organization, as is the case when you're Miss America, the need to look the part is obvious. But make no mistake about it, almost every single job or advanced opportunity you seek, your ability to be an effective "face" of the organization will be evaluated.

This is exactly what is meant by "being the face" of

the organization. Let's call it "face value." No, I do not mean the attractiveness of your face (the world is not a beauty contest), but you only help yourself when you recognize that by visually exhibiting the sophistication, organization, values, and substance of a company, you become an even more valuable asset. Some roles actually have this kind of language detailed in the job description, particularly roles around sales, liaison, or representative. But trust that this "face value" component is not limited just to roles that identify it as a defined part of the job. It is wise to presume that *every* role will be enhanced by your ability to bolster the overall company brand by maintaining an appearance that is consistent with what the company strives to represent.

"Face value" is not and will never be a substitute for performing well in your role. Simply looking the part might get you through the door, but it won't keep you inside. And you can forget about moving up in any sustainable way if you do not couple your efforts around physical presentation with consistency, discipline, and capability. But the reason "face value" should be a professional priority is because of its immediacy. Visually presenting in a way that aligns with a company's goals and branding will immediately give you early consideration. Before you open your mouth, you have their attention, so now keeping that attention is up to you. That is where you have to be consistent with your style and substance.

For Haglund, she knew that to visually present as Miss America she needed to make some adjustments. She knew she possessed academic achievement, and was knowledge-able and passionate about her platform of eating disorders, and was very talented as a ballet dancer, but simply possessing all of the components of a great Miss America wasn't enough. She needed to look like Miss America. Haglund's challenge was her age. She possessed a maturity way past her eighteen years, but she was competing against women in their early twenties. The Miss America Organization was clear about the fact that they were hiring a women for a year-long job of being an ambassador who would be tasked with fundraising, speaking engagements, meetings with elected officials, and numerous other professional obligations. Miss America is not simply a beauty queen, she is a businesswoman. While the technical age range to compete is eighteen to twenty-four, very few eighteen year olds are crowned as Miss America because there can be a presumption that a girl that age wouldn't be "ready." Haglund understood that she needed to create a visual presentation that conveyed "readiness," so she selected suits and hair and makeup styling that played up her ability to handle business. It is important not to take this step too far and end up looking like a little girl trying to play dress-up or be Corporate Barbie. But it is savvy to think of ways to convey particular attributes that you want to highlight when positioning yourself for a role. In Haglund's case, she chose to highlight her business readiness, but other examples could be demonstrating a youthful sense of style for a creative job, a very polished look for a more corporate environment, or a modern look in the tech field.

And never leave home without your personal style. Always give yourself permission to add your personal flairs of femininity, energy, and personality in your look. This process of developing "face value" is to complement your personal style, not substitute it. Haglund showed her understanding of this concept when she decided to chop her hair off shortly after her crowning moment. While titleholders traditionally wear their hair long, Haglund decided she wanted to participate in the current trend of a chic choppy bob. She initially received push back from the organization and from fans as she toured the country, but she felt confident in her personal style choice and never saw the haircut as undermining her ability to convey the glamour and femininity associated with being Miss America. Because she owned the decision and the look, she was successful in selling it as brand appropriate, and it even injected a dose of freshness that is often lacking in the perception of titleholders.

I'd say I know the pageant system well, and I know how important image and branding are to the organization, but I've also known Haglund for a long time. I would describe her as incredibly mature, forward thinking, and thoughtful, and as someone who is very concerned with being authentic to herself and authentic to her age. I asked her how she stayed true to herself and conveyed power, authority, confidence, and being in command in jeans and a more fashion-forward top with a cute bob cut, instead of something more formal like some would expect. Haglund explained, "So, so much of it comes down to body language and communication skills, because how you carry yourself—first of all, if we're just talking from the fashion perspective—how you carry yourself in an outfit, whatever it is, is the determinant of how people perceive you in that fashion choice by far, especially when you're doing events in places like New York City or Los Angeles or San Francisco or cities where a lot more things are accepted. But even if you're in a place that has more norms about what people should wear like the South or some parts of the Midwest, the way that you hold yourself and carry yourself really says a lot about you and controls the way that other people perceive you." Haglund has advice for those of us who may hear her but may not know what that means, who may not know how to better represent the woman we want to be: "First of all, practice putting on a lot of different styles of clothing. What do you feel best in? When do you stand up the straightest? Posture is a huge, huge thing. I'm so cognizant of this because of my dance background, but when a woman stands up straight, puts her shoulders back, sticks out her chest . . . whatever size it may be, and not that it's about your physical anatomy, but it's about holding your head high and putting your shoulders back that studies have proven—there's a Ted Talk on this—actually increases levels of adrenalin in your body and decreases levels of cortisol. Cortisol is a stress hormone, and adrenalin and dopamine are feel good hormones. [Same advice] if you're going into an interview or some stressful situation. Power pose, go stand in a way so that it actually affects the chemicals in your body. And you can then project that."

Haglund continued, "In the study, they showed that the interviewers . . . were more likely to hire the candidates who did the power posing. So women can take a lot from that. People read body language signs before they read anything else, so . . . practice wearing different styles, wear modern, wear something more trendy, and don't follow the trend if it doesn't look good on you and if you don't feel good in it, don't wear it. So try a lot of different things. See how you feel in each one. Carry that feeling into whatever social situation that it is through posture. And throughout [it] repeat a mantra."

One of the mantras Haglund used when she was recovering from her eating disorder, when she was dealing with a lot of negative feelings and always shaming her body, she used to tell her thoughts to "Go to hell!" I love it! Like all of us, even Miss America experiences negative feelings and has challenges, but the difference between her and women who don't succeed is that she didn't let the negativity keep her in a place of defeat.

After all of her experiences, I wanted to know if Haglund had any advice or caution around leveraging your look for a power ascent, and if there's a situation where you go too far. She shared, "The thing is that people who are successful, and I mean not only successful professionally but personally, and [who are] okay with who they are, are people that are the full package because I know, and I'm sure that you've known, many beautiful people who are extremely empty on the inside. And there are people that might not be on the world scale at ten. Might be a seven or a six, but because they emanate so much inner beauty and confidence and 'it' factor, that they become more beautiful to the people around them. So obviously there's a scale. Here's something that I discovered on my own quest for perfection . . . it doesn't matter how much you starve yourself or how much you diet or how many perfect foods you eat or what size of jeans you are, there's going to be someone out there to whose beauty standard you don't conform. And so they don't find you attractive or beautiful or worth it. And [what] I learned . . . is that you [have to] accept your beauty—and everyone has something beautiful about them that they were born with. [For example,] my mom has beautiful long eyelashes, she's Italian, she gave me beautiful long eyelashes. [She] had super long legs, she gave me super long legs. There are other things that she didn't give me, [but] that's enough, that's okay. It's [about] focusing on the things that you do have, and loving and accepting the beautiful things that you do have and being confident in those and magnifying those.

"And because everyone has something different to offer, and I'll tell you, you can be the most beautiful person in the world, and if you're not confident in accepting inside yourself, you're not going to appear as the most beautiful person in the world to the people around you, and that's why beauty really, and using your aesthetic, is about the full package. You're not going to be able to utilize what you've been given naturally if you don't have what comes from the inside. That's what I tell young girls when I speak to them. If you don't love yourself on the inside you [might get to your goals], and you're still going to hate yourself. You're still not going to be confident, and people are still not going to want to be around you. And you're not going to be successful because you're not beautiful on the inside."

Haglund's is an incredibly purposeful journey and it is critical that as you embark upon the process of tailoring your presentation to the world, you always keep in mind the ultimate purpose. That ultimate purpose is to best position yourself for the powerful role you desire and deserve. Losing sight is easy to do, but takes you completely off course, and you end up lost in a world of superficiality that is all consuming. When done effectively, this pretty power play should become so second nature that you don't have to give as much thought or energy to it, and there's no chance of compromising yourself along the way.

CHAPTER 9

THE EVOLUTION OF PRETTY POWER

With Insight from Judge Jeanine Pirro

"When I started, you have to understand, there were no role models for me. If it were today, I probably would not be as constrained by my inner concerns about being a woman."
—JUDGE JEANINE PIRRO

Judge Jeanine Pirro has no subtlety with her *Pretty Powerful* philosophy: "One of the things that I despise are women who use their sexuality to get ahead in business or in the marketplace. I despise them. They are cockroaches as far as I'm concerned. They make it harder for other women, and I don't really care what the short-term gain is for them. For some, there's a long-term gain. All they have to do is just screw their way to get to the top. And if they're good they'll stay on top. But these women are cockroaches. They're all over, trust me. And I have fought very hard to make sure that there's never a question regarding my seriousness, my professionalism. And I think that women who do it and who think that other people don't know are just kidding themselves, because everyone knows. The one, you want to say, cautionary tale (I've not been in that situation, nor would I allow it to happen) for these women is that it may be a short-term gain, it may be a long-term gain, but you're a pathetic creature. That's all. I feel very strongly about it. I see it all the time."

It's clear to anyone that Judge Pirro (judge, prosecutor, 2006 Republican nominee for New York attorney general, turned legal analyst and television personality) has a strong point of view and doesn't mince words. Before Judge Pirro arrived at Fox News, she did not even own a dress. The fact epitomizes an old school train of thought. As the judge tells it, "Even when I was going to black tie events, I would wear a jacket with a skirt or a jacket with pants. I was always covered up. I always felt that I had to be covered up."

I asked the judge where that need or expectation was coming from. Judge Pirro shared, "There were a couple of places. Number one, it was intrinsic. I knew that I was in a man's world, and I was always surrounded by men. For me, I was a girl who grew up in a small town in upstate New York. I worked in a dairy, was very wholesome, and went to church. It was all about school and family. When I went to law school, there was a lot of criticism because I went to law school in 1972. I graduated in 1975. When I went to high school—I skipped my last year of high school—but when I went to high school I wore a uniform. It was with a jacket. And then, when I went to law school, it was a different time when people were resentful—that you were taking a guy's place."

126

To look at the judge today, she is an ageless vision of beauty and femininity that typically wears a collection of the latest Herve Leger signature bandage dress in a rainbow of colors. But it's important to note that the judge came out of law school in 1975, a time when the legal practice was completely male dominated. Thankfully, today women make up around 48 percent of law school graduates, compared to only 10 percent in Judge Pirro's class.

When the Judge went to the district attorney's (DA) office, she was just the second woman—the first woman was in Appeals, and no one really saw her and she recalled palpable resentment toward her that she was taking a man's spot in the law school class. The judge makes it clear that her expectation to be "covered" was derived from a need to survive a judgmental environment. "So," she said, "I just kind of felt the most appropriate was a jacket. I wore horn rimmed glasses. No makeup." Judge Pirro was not into makeup. It just was not her thing. She remembers, "The first time I went to Bergdorf Goodman, I said to the lady behind the counter, (whispers) 'I need some blush.' She said to me, 'Honey, you need more than blush.' And *that* was the beginning!"

Like many women, Judge Pirro simply wasn't that into makeup at the time, but for the judge that shopping experience was a wake-up call. For her to have a more polished look, she needed to make more effort around her makeup routine and look. This is not a mandate to pile on tons of makeup in an effort to hide your natural looks; quite the contrary. Effective makeup is enough to enhance your best features, create illusions around anything you're not thrilled about, and make you feel like your best self. Makeup that serves to hide your face or essentially shame your natural looks misses the entire point and is counter-productive. Again, the entire point of tapping into your pretty power is to make you feel fully confident as you enter professional spaces so that you can present and perform as your best self, even when that performance requires some tough decision-making and ability.

When Judge Pirro first went to court, she was the first woman to prosecute a murder case in the history of Westchester County, New York. She had to fight to get into that courtroom, and she recalls it felt like "Women can't go for the jugular." So, she always wore a pinstriped skirt suit with a white cotton shirt, and she said, "I used to wear the bow ties." The first day of court, Judge Pirro says she "wore a pinstripe suit, and then it was, navy, and then it was red because that was a power color." For summation, she says, "It was always black. That was just my choice because my cases were the ugliest—they were homicides, child abuse homicides, that kind of thing."

Traditionally, trying high-stakes and typically gruesome murder cases was just not something women were seen as capable of. Therefore when deciding what to wear that initial day of court was important to the judge. She recognized her attire as an opportunity to start to reshape the narrative around what a woman could handle in the courtroom. She knew she needed to project authority, strength, and power. She selected a series of structured skirt suits including pinstripe, navy, black, and red, because red is known as a power color.

After a successful career as a prosecutor, the judge decided to further her power ascent. This time she sought a seat on the bench. She ran to become the first woman judge in Westchester County. When she mounted her campaign she would hear echoing questions about whether a woman was strong enough to enforce the toughest laws, could a woman *really* sentence someone to life in prison? Or would she be too soft? As a way to visually protest this sexist stereotype, the judge wore a uniform of suits. The suits represented intensity, strength, and, in a way, masculinity. Since the presumption was that to be an effective judge you needed to be a man, perhaps subconsciously, Judge Pirro committed to wearing the male associated power suit even when it was ninety degrees out, all in an effort to show her toughness and ability to be just like "the guys."

When Judge Pirro decided to run for judge in 1989, there was a lot of criticism she says, "Because I was a woman." She would be the first woman in the history of the county to be a county judge. She was faced with "Are women that strong?," "They really can't do it, she can't sentence someone to life." But Judge Pirro had on her suit of armor. She says, "I would go to the park in a suit." The suit and the jacket conveyed the seriousness and conservativeness of her strength and her ability to get the job done. When other women were outside of that dress code, Judge Pirro says, "I would look at other women and think to myself, that's unprofessional. For me, it was strength. It delivered a message. And it was my coat of armor. I was going to war. No matter where I was, if I walked into that courtroom, it was war. And occasionally, you'd get a judge now and then who would comment on your nice legs, this and that. So I always understood that as the only woman who was trying these cases—and they were all male judges—you did not want to reduce yourself because you were different enough. I remember the gasp when I walked in a courtroom and the judge said,

'And prosecuting this case will be Jeanine Pirro.' I kind of stood up and in unison, all of the prospective jurors went, 'Oooooh.' So then, I run for office, and I win. I become a judge. Talk about a coat of armor—the robe. I didn't like [the county's] robe, so I went to Scaasi and he designed my robe. So there was always the girl in me. Trust me, there was always that girl in me."

I always wondered if judges are wearing fun outfits under their robes, so I'm sure others wondered as well. I asked the judge how she reconciled that. "Yeah, a lot of men always wanted to know what was under those robes and it pissed me off," she says. She continued, "But it was very easy, my career was number one in my life. I could be pretty anytime I wanted, but the fact that I was a woman, and looked at as a young woman, who probably couldn't do it. When I was assistant DA, I remember a guy coming into the New Rochelle local court saying, 'I want to speak to the assistant to the DA.' I said, 'That's me.' 'I want to speak to the DA's assistant.' 'The assistant DA, that's me.' 'I want to talk to a man! Don't you get it?' It was unbelievable. But I understood that it was part of the image. There was a turning point—that robe. And I would wear pretty things under it. One of my robes I actually lined in pink inside, so I could sit on the bench and inhale, 'Ah' and no one would ever know it." The judge felt her femininity.

She successfully ran for her judgeship in 1989, but I won't pretend that many of those same antiquated and sexist stereotypes about women in law and on the bench don't persist today. The difference is that today there are so many more women demonstrating daily that not only can women do the jobs traditionally held by men, but many of us do them better than our male counterparts.

As such, I submit that women have completely earned the right to embrace whatever appearance they want in their professional capacities, including getting rid of the male emulated power suit if they want to. Now, don't get me wrong, there is absolutely nothing wrong with a woman choosing to don a flattering and comfortable power suit if she wants to. The key here is choice. Gone are the days when (similar to how Judge Pirro felt) a competent and powerful woman is internally compelled to sacrifice her personal comfort and style in an effort to debunk ridiculous sexist stereotypes questioning women's ability to be powerful, strong, and effective.

I still remember the first day I entered the courtroom to be sworn into practice in the state of North Carolina. I had been in many courtrooms during my experience as a law student, but this was different. I was wearing a black skirt suit, nude hosiery and black pumps. I waited in the back of the courtroom sitting beside my mother, who would hold the Bible as I was sworn in. The judge, The Honorable Yvonne Mims-Evans recognized me sitting in the back, because I had attended elementary school with her daughter. Although I had not come from the privileged world of esteemed attorneys and other professionals, Judge Evans always treated me with kindness, but today there was a different look in her eye. The look was filled with respect, but as she recited (and had me repeat) the attorney's oath, she charged me with the enormous responsibility and privilege to uphold our constitution and zealously advocate for the rights of every single person or entity I represented. From that day forward, every time I walk into a courtroom, I also am going to war. As an attorney I am very literally a representative, and everything about me, including my appearance, conveys a message about my credibility, my preparation, and my competence. Most important is that the conclusions drawn about my appearance don't only affect me, they affect the person or company that I'm advocating on behalf of. As Judge Pirro accurately put it, us women holding positions of power must have our coat of armor.

When Judge Pirro ascended to the bench, she possessed a very bold coat of armor, her black judicial robe. In an effort to reconcile her true spirit with her assigned garment, Judge Pirro had a robe custom designed for her, complete with a pink lining. Particularly awesome about the pink lining is that no one could see it, but she felt the femininity and power that radiated from it. Taking the initiative to give herself that customized detail to her coat of armor was a total power play. As she sat on the bench day after day, hearing case after case, she was empowered by her own sense of self, style, and confidence.

When Judge Pirro made the decision to step off the bench to run for DA she had to hold a press conference because her opponent said that she wasn't a good mother because "who would be taking care of my children." And meanwhile, the judge says, "He had three kids, his wife was pregnant with a fourth, and she delivered during the campaign." She laughs, "But—and I couldn't say this—I couldn't say we had three live-ins." The judge had it covered. When Judge Pirro speaks of going "to war," as a practicing attorney, I know exactly what she's talking about.

Adding to her long list of "firsts," she successfully became the first woman to be elected district attorney of Westchester County. It was after this milestone achievement that the judge started integrating color into her wardrobe. She began wearing bold shades of blue, pink, and green. Judge Pirro says, "I introduced color because I could do it. I'd earned it. I'd proven myself. I'd been elected as the first woman county judge, the first woman DA, I won every felony case I ever tried. It worked. It just worked for me." She felt she'd earned the right not to be bound by anyone's expectations of what a "prosecutor" or "powerful attorney" should look like. She also continued to wear the suits, but she went to Chanel, as she says, "Really high end."

People took notice. Literarily, *People* magazine named her one of its "50 Most Beautiful People" in 1997. The magazine called her and said, "We picked you as one of the fifty most beautiful women in the world." Judge Pirro said, "Yeah, right, who is it? My assistant had called me, and she said, 'Judge'—they always call me 'Judge'— 'there's someone on the phone.' Long story short, they said, 'We want to photograph you.' And I said, 'Well, I'm going to be in Israel next week, and I didn't plan on [being photographed], what do you want me to wear?' They said, 'Don't worry about it, we'll bring the clothes.' And they flew to Israel, the photographer, and makeup, hair, the whole thing, in Jerusalem. And they did it. It was beautiful. But they put me in a . . . brown dress with a very simple thin jacket, no lapels, just kind of hung."

This changed a lot for her. There was a lot of controversy about whether or not Judge Pirro should have agreed to do that shoot. The judge felt, "It was just one picture," but on the local TV news there was a story about whether she should have done the shoot with *People*. In the local newspapers, Judge Pirro had some support with readers saying, "Why not?", "She's pretty, she's beautiful, why not?", "What's she got to hide?", and "I'm proud of her." That is when the judge felt, "Oh, my God, it's time, I can turn. That's when I turned to the colors. But I still never got away from the jacket. Never, never."

Unfortunately and unsurprisingly, the judge got slack for appearing in the magazine. The local news criticized her decision to appear in something deemed so superficial. But to her pleasant surprise, there was also a chorus of community members that wrote op-eds in the local newspapers showing their support for the judge's decision to model for the list. Many applauded her for being beautiful, bold, and brilliant. It was a turn of the tide and she felt it.

I asked Judge Pirro if she had it to do it over again, coming out of law school today, would she go straight for color and what expression she wanted to make to the world, or would she bide her time. Would she approach it with as much caution and consideration? "When I started," she said, "You have to understand, there were no role models for me. If it were today, I probably would not be as constrained by my inner concerns about being a woman in a level playing field for myself. But I would have been conservative, no doubt about it. No doubt about it."

When asked if she wishes she had taken the liberties to incorporate color, abandon the structured jackets, and further embrace her femininity in her appearance earlier in her career, she answered with pure perspective. Without feeling such a heavy burden to reshape narratives around women in positions of power, she wouldn't have been as concerned with projecting such a clear image that focused so much on divorcing herself from femininity. But as things were in the genesis of her legal career, she proudly stands by her choices to use every opportunity she had to convey a message of equality with males, even if it meant replicating their style at times. But the judge also points out that times have changed for the better. Today's women are in no way immune from gender stereotypes around our professional abilities or mental toughness when it comes to certain professions, but because of the deliberate steps taken by Judge Pirro and countless other women who worked to make it clear that regardless of what we looked like, we were as strong, prepared, and capable of leading in courtrooms, boardrooms, or Congress as our male counterparts, many women today can exercise incredible freedom around our professional appearance.

Over time, Judge Pirro feels she earned the right to be more expressive and individual. She said, "I think that was a significant part, but it was a societal acceptance. I saw that loud and clear. And I remember my public information officer, who was a great guy, he said, 'Judge, you can do it, you can do it.' And I was like, 'I don't know, David, I don't know.' And then, I did something for Calvin Klein. Something called Significant Women—I think it was 1998. They had the most significant women in the nation, and they dressed us up. So it was me, a famous doctor, and then there was Ann Richards, the governor from Texas. Then there was Bebe Neuwirth in her world. And Reba McIntyre. There were like fifteen of us. They wanted me in a gown, and David wouldn't let me do it. (That's my public information officer.) He said, 'She will wear a suit.' "

CHAPTER 10

Brand Equity

"I am a businesswoman who goes to work every single day."

—TYRA BANKS

. . . Says the supermodel.

A photogenic face, fierce walk, height, and fabulous fashion. That's what many of us probably think are the sole requirements of being a successful model. I mean, a model's purpose is to convey an image, a look that grabs attention, influences the onlooker, and persuades us to want what the model has. Selling a look could be seen as the definition of leveraging "pretty," but, as I've asserted throughout this conversation, that high-priced pretty package alone (even in our image-obsessed culture) will never be enough to achieve the maximum level of power as a woman in today's world.

Today, any "about" Internet search for Tyra Banks is

sure to bring up information detailing this $90 million net worth businesswoman's roles of producer, American television personality, and author. You're likely to find mention that she's even recently completed an Owner/President Management (OPM) program at Harvard Business School, adding to credentials she clearly doesn't "need" with the level of success she's already achieved. But most of us still think of and refer to Tyra Banks by the title "supermodel."

Her climb to the top started with an active career as a model between 1991–2005. The Inglewood, California, born, 5'10" looker began modeling at the early age of fifteen and became the first African American woman to be featured on the covers of *GQ* and the *Sports Illustrated* Swimsuit Issue (twice). She also gained popularity for being a Victoria's Secret Angel from 1997 to 2005. A decade into her career, Banks was one of the top-earning models in the world.

But Banks had something else that other models during that time did not. She had the type of life experiences that build character, and she was smart. She had capitalized on her aesthetic and pretty package in the most literal way a woman can (by monetizing her image as a working model), but she was intelligent enough to know that would never be enough to really achieve the height of her potential. Banks is often quoted as saying very simply, "You can't model for the rest of your life, so it is important to diversify your career." And that's what she did.

In 2003, Banks created and produced the reality television series "America's Next Top Model" (ANTM), the longest-running fashion reality TV series in history. The series ran under her creative control and with her as the star panel host for twenty-two "cycles" (short seasons) before being cancelled in 2015. Then in December 2016 (with just a one-year hiatus), the show was revived and brought back (still under Banks's executive leadership) with the new host Rita Ora.

Season twenty-three of ANTM is back, with a new group of twenty-eight aspiring models who are competing for the coveted title of America's Next Top Model. This season, however, is being loud and clear about what it really takes to be a powerhouse as a woman in the world. This season is teaching the lesson that I've been asserting this entire book, that it takes capitalizing on our dual assets as women. This season's theme (to my applause) is "Business, Brand, Boss." That season opening episode title is also the concept that Banks is enforcing to these young women (and the audience) in every single head-to-head challenge in every single episode: to be a boss as a woman, you have to maximize your brand *and* be smart at business.

Since we're talking business, it's time to address the all-important business principles of appreciation and depreciation. Pretty power depreciates. At some point the value begins to decrease. Some would even classify the value assigned to beauty as an exponential depreciation asset, meaning it decreases at a rate proportional to its current value. Pretty power depreciates every day.

To be clear, some women are fortunate enough to maintain and even increase their beautiful appearance over the years (see the primer for tips on how to do this). You can moisturize, exfoliate, and avoid the sun all you want, but none of us can ultimately defeat Father Time. Time catches up with all of us, even the most intentional pretty preservationists. There comes a point in every woman's life (if she lives long enough) when her looks begin to fade; it's nature! The pageant community is so preoccupied with the phenomenon that we even created a deadline, we call it "aging out" and it tends to happen around twenty-seven years old in that world (no pressure!). I submit that deadline is quite the overreaction to the fear of a woman's aesthetic depreciation, but you get the point.

Even women who sincerely are not (or claim not to be) concerned with their appearance are keenly aware when this shift starts. But the depreciation of our looks hits those of us who rely more heavily on our appearance for our business success (television broadcasters, actresses, models, performers, etc.) much harder. The issue of "aging out" isn't as hard of a line as it is in pageants, but it starts to creep into the psyche and realities of many women in our forties, fifties, and sixties. When Banks professes that she can't model all of her life, this is exactly what she's talking about. Obviously as a model this rings more true for her industry than most other women's, but it rings true nonetheless.

This is where the coupling of the substance becomes imperative. Pretty power is still a very important and valuable tool to be maximized at every opportunity; however, it can never stand alone (as argued throughout the entire book) but also pretty power will never have the longevity of substance. Therefore, having substance to go alongside your pretty power is a requirement for professional success, but if you want to be really smart about it, it's a good idea to double down on your substantive credentials while in the midst of your power ascent.

This is particularly smart because the pretty power is

most valuable early on and best used to get you in doors (particularly useful early in your career). After you're in the door you should not disregard your appearance, instead you should make every effort to maintain and improve it, if possible. But the fact remains that at some point continuing to invest time and resources primarily in your pretty is just bad business because you'll hit that depreciation point and now you're losing instead of gaining on your investment. Instead, at some point you must choose where and how you're investing your time and resources for self-improvement. The smarter play is to make the larger investment in your substantive portfolio (ex: Banks obtaining that Harvard business certificate) because the substance will sustain and appreciate over time. In short, invest in pretty power and substance on the front end and over time—as you must make choices around how and where you invest your time and resources between the two areas—elect to primarily invest in growing your substantive component because it will yield a better and longer return. Since pretty power does depreciate at some point, once you've arrived at that point the stronger business strategy is to further (I say further because you've been developing it the entire time) develop the appreciable asset: your substance.

The brand must be driven by the substance. Just look at any *Time* magazine "Most Influential" issue or *Forbes* magazine "Most Powerful Women" list and pop culture queens Beyoncé and Taylor Swift are at the top. These ladies were doing well enough just coasting on their looks and talents but opted to tap into their pretty power to become global business powerhouses.

Beyoncé and Taylor Swift both made *Forbes*'s "Most

Powerful Women in the World" list for 2015. The net worth of Beyoncé is estimated to be $450 million. Taylor Swift is reported to be worth around $200 million. These mega-millions are not solely the result of album sales or concert tickets. While these pop stars are performers by trade, a vast portion of their fortunes are the result of massive brand appeal, image control, and marketing. The thoughtful nature of these women's actions cumulated in unprecedented financial and business gains that beautifully illustrate the effectiveness of a dual-prong strategy.

Beyoncé has spent her life excelling at performance. Her development into a world class businesswoman is an excellent case study for the strategy of employing image to masterfully leverage success to the next level. The fact that Beyoncé is a particularly beautiful woman should not be ignored, of course that helps, a lot. But her business ascent must take into account her precise and deliberate control of that beautiful image. Let's face it, Beyoncé is not the first beautiful face to sing and dance very well. But her ability to transition from traditional performer to business mogul is evidence of the effectiveness of her intentional displays of image paying off in large dividends. Beyoncé's aesthetic is one of ultra glam, often with long, lush blonde locks cascading down her butter-scotch complexion. Her performance attire progressively embraced her sexuality—including leotards, sky-high stilettos, and ultra-feminine bustiers. Her impeccable makeup is not surprising given her profession, but even for a pop star, we rarely see Beyoncé minus her perfect face, even when she is walking the streets of Los Angeles or sitting courtside at a Brooklyn Nets basketball game.

It is no small detail that part of the appeal of Beyoncé's

image is the cultural broadness of her appeal. Part genetic and part engineered, her aesthetic is racially ambiguous enough to cross over to women of all ethnic groups. While she remains a black woman, her look becomes aspirational to women who are black, white, Latina, Asian, Native American, and others. This becomes particularly powerful in global marketing: because of her ambiguous image, she is incredibly desirable by corporations from every part of the world. Beyoncé is a commercial powerhouse in America, Asia, Africa, Europe, and beyond.

What is ultimately created is a carefully crafted look of never-ending femininity, glamour, and sexiness. That look is the perfect marketing tool for a slew of endorsements including a $50 million deal with Pepsi. The Pepsi deal was remarkable because it included a specific clause that granted broad creative control to Beyoncé. In a statement to the *New York Times*, Beyoncé expressed the importance of her creative control, "Pepsi embraces creativity and understands that artists evolve. As a businesswoman, this allows me to work with a lifestyle brand with no compromise and without sacrificing my creativity." The preservation of that creative control is not accidental. That control is completely necessary for a woman who has a notorious reputation for meticulous management over every photograph, video, and social media image. Even if that need for control started as a part of an artist's vision, it certainly ends up being an integral part of a highly successful business model.

The cultivation and maintenance of such a deliberately universal look was likely a strategy in the case of Beyoncé and some others. Even my own aesthetic is built around my ability to be heard by broad audiences so that I can have maximum impact distributing my messages around politics, culture, and social justice. For me this is an application of the lesson I learned as a child actress appearing in commercials—the broader you can appeal, the more likely your message or product is to resonate and sell.

But what works for me or Beyoncé is not the only way to be intentional and successful around personal aesthetic cultivation. You absolutely do not need to have a universal or "traditionally commercially appealing" look to thrive. It doesn't have to be about appealing to the masses, it's about understanding and accepting your own look with confidence, and finding the best way to embrace it and capitalize on it. Pretty power is not one size fits all and there is no singular definition of what "pretty" even is. When coming up with the title of this book there was concern around "Pretty Powerful" because so many people interpret that in an arcane, narrow, oppressive way that leaves only a select few feeling included in the definition. I utterly reject that and fought to keep the title *Pretty Powerful* because I wholeheartedly believe we need to forcefully reject that stale old narrative that permits other people to dictate what "pretty" is. Sure, it can be traditional, universally accepted looks of flawless complexion, long locks, and pearly white teeth. But it is also beautiful textures of kink, full and healthy figures, and bright gap-toothed smiles. We can embrace and cultivate looks that play broadly or narrowly or customize them anywhere in between. The point is, pretty is what we want it to be and we hold the power to "sell it" as such; whatever look makes us comfortable, proud and empowered. That is the entire point of pretty power.

Beyoncé, in addition to her *Forbes* titles, previously sat

atop *Time* magazine's "Most Influential 100 People" list. I appeared in a Fox News Channel segment to discuss the reasons why *Time* was absolutely right to rank the pop star above the likes of the sitting president of the United States, the U.S. attorney general, two consecutive U.S. secretaries of state, and a U.S. senator. And those were just the political power players. I had previously appeared on Bill O'Reilly's show to highlight the problems I had with much of Beyoncé's hyper-sexual imagery, but it is impossible to argue against her influence. Classical beacons of female power like Hillary Clinton, Oprah, Sheryl Sandberg (who wrote the explainer accompanying the pop star's lovely photo) failed to make the magazine's list, or fell far below the glamorous singer.

This outcome really made me think about how our modern society defines influence—and ultimately power. Particularly, it is important to acknowledge the new definition of female power and from where it most purely derives. I am hard pressed to find any person more beloved, and who holds more ability to impact society at large, than Beyoncé. She is a successful recording artist, a celebrated performer, and she possesses physical beauty that makes her the face of choice for major commercial campaigns ranging from L'Oréal to Pepsi. But those qualities alone cannot explain the hold this one woman has on our entire society. There are many beautiful, talented performers in the world and they are not all on the cover of *Time*'s Most Influential 100 issue. So what is it about this woman who commands the attention of men and women, young and old, and the entire racial spectrum?

The answer to that question becomes the new definition of the modern day female power source. It relies on a delicate balance of sex appeal and substance. The balance of those two elements remains critical in the ascent to power.

Taylor Swift is another pop star who has greatly multiplied her fortune with brand expansion. At twenty-five, Swift was the youngest person on the 2015 *Forbes*'s "Most Powerful Women" list. The singer-songwriter completed her transition from country darling to pop superstar with the launch of the album "1989," the top release of 2014 with over 3.6 million copies sold—making her one of only three artists with a platinum album that year. That new state of affairs is partly due to the rise of streaming, a distribution system of which Swift has become one of the most outspoken critics, pulling her music from Spotify and forcing Apple to pay artists during their service's free trial period. Talk about a major power move.

Swift's wealth—derived from record sales and touring, as well as her own fragrance line and property holdings—gives her the luxury of not having to walk the traditional music industry path where the artist is last in line for control and power. And she uses that power. Viewed as both an advocate for artists and a game-changer—almost no other pop star could have made Apple Music roll over—the twenty-five year-old Pennsylvanian is arguably the world's most powerful female music star. *Time* magazine, Bloomberg, and *Businessweek* ran cover stories to that effect: "Taylor Swift Is the Music Industry," said Bloomberg, while *Time* headlined its piece "The Power of Taylor Swift." The other contender for that status is the aforementioned Beyoncé.

Swift's ten-year career has reached a junction where critical approval, commercial success, and cultural impact have coalesced. She is an influencer—the sort of celebrity who can say, "My hope for the future, not just in the music industry, but in every young girl I meet . . . is that they all realize their worth and ask for it." And the world will listen. That is incredibly powerful.

Beyoncé, Swift, and so many other thriving women in today's society are brilliant, and most important, consistent, in their maintenance of their command of the dual elements that are responsible for their power dominance. While these celebrity examples might seem hyper in nature, they are very clear models of what, when done at their optimum level, the balance of substantive capability and aesthetic control can produce.

CHAPTER 11

TRUTH & CONSEQUENCES: SEXUAL HARASSMENT

When Gretchen Carlson sued then-CEO of Fox News Roger Ailes, the world stopped. Certainly the cable news and mass media worlds were shaken to their core as the creator and visionary of the most successful cable news network was being brought to his knees. Carlson started a very important conversation about sexual harassment, one that grew to fever pitch during the remainder of the 2016 presidential election season. Between the claims against Ailes, the *Access Hollywood* tapes showing GOP nominee Donald Trump suggesting that because he's famous he can grab women by their genitals, and lingering claims about former president Bill Clinton's sexually abusive behavior, America was having its most attentive moment concerning sexual harassment since Clarence Thomas's judicial confirmation hearing in 1991.

While the events that have led to us having to reckon with this very painful topic are completely regrettable, I greatly appreciate the opportunity to address the very important issue of sexual harassment. This topic was always going to be addressed in this book because it would have been patently irresponsible for me to write this book which so directly asserts many theories around women's appearance and not address the possible unintended consequence of sexual harassment. The 2016 presidential election and snowballing of accusations around the Fox News Channel only serve to emphasize why this issue so desperately needs attention. Much of what I am asserting about women making a conscious and deliberate effort around the way they look in an effort to exert and possess power, could be confusing for some people. For some, the suggestion could be interpreted as some kind of slippery slope that leads to an invitation of women being objectified, sexually harassed, or even sexually assaulted. I want to make it unequivocally clear that there is nothing any woman can wear and no way she can style herself that will ever justify her being insulted, harassed, or assaulted in any way.

In a "Daily Beast" column entitled "Roger Ailes Sexually Harassed Me: I Thought I Was the First and Last," Shelley Ross appears to suggest this type of thinking. "You only have to look at most of the women on air at Fox to believe they are, at least, partners in their own objectification." Ross, in her scathing critique of the "women on air at Fox" is engaging in the type of victim shaming that only exacerbates the ignorant misunderstanding that often plagues the issue of sexual harassment. It's sad when women turn on each other, misplace responsibility, and confuse a proactive professional strategy as an invitation to be sexually harassed. As I tweeted in 2012, there is no uniform for rape, and likewise there is no uniform for sexual harassment.

To conclude that women freely exercising their choice to appear in the way that they feel comfortable, appropriate, and which maximizes their professional role is "self-objectification" is a slap in the face of the work of the feminist movement. A huge part of feminist theory is about women being free to choose to exist in this world on their own terms. For some of us, that includes styling and carrying ourselves in a way that is particularly glamorous. I fully understand that that is not desirable or comfortable for every woman, nor does it have to be. There is no singular way to look feminine, professional, or well put together. Choice is key here. But shaming women that do elect to exhibit a particular aesthetic and then blaming them for the tortious actions of someone else, is a huge part of the problem of why we haven't made the strides around sexual harassment that we should.

Sexual harassment tends to be completely misunderstood. The modern definition evolved in the early 1970s. Sexual harassment is bullying or coercion of a sexual nature or the unwelcome or inappropriate promise of rewards in exchange for sexual favors, which is known as quid pro quo. In most legal contexts, sexual harassment is illegal as defined by the U.S. Equal Employment Opportunity Commission, "It is unlawful to harass a person (an applicant or employee) because of that person's sex."

What can muddy the waters of strictly defining sexual harassment is that while laws surrounding sexual harassment exist, they generally do not prohibit simple teasing, offhand comments, or minor isolated incidents. Therefore, whether a comment is considered sexual harassment has to be put in particular context. Also, in the workplace, harassment may be considered illegal when it is so frequent or severe that it creates a hostile or offensive work environment, or when it results in an adverse employment decision (such as the victim being fired or demoted, or when the victim decides to quit the job). The legal and social understandings of sexual harassment vary.

Do all of these elements of frequency, pattern, or severity need to be present for behavior or commentary to constitute sexual harassment? Certainly not. But it does leave most instances of sexual harassment claims in need of unique analysis. What might feel like sexual harassment to one person, might not meet that threshold for someone else and coming up with uniform standards, while necessary, remains difficult. For example, an executive tells a female host that she will do exceptionally well working on a show and that she has great legs. Is that sexual harassment, a *Mad Men* era ignorant comment, a compliment, a sexist comment, a relevant assessment of one part of what that host is contributing to the broadcast, or a subtle implication that if her legs become "less great" her job could be in jeopardy? I suspect if you ask three different people what category the example falls into you will get three different answers.

This is not a permission slip for people to start saying or doing anything they want. Instead, it's an honest analysis of how different people construe the scenarios differently, and they should be allowed to. While I'm not interested in a quid pro quo scenario where my professional development is dependent on putting up with unwanted sexual advances, I do not feel harassed if someone in the workplace says I have nice legs, or that my dress fits well, or that my hairstyle is perfect for my face. I work in television so those comments all have tangible value in what

I'm offering in my role as an on-air host and analyst. But I've also held professional positions long before my television career. The leg comment would feel weird and inappropriate if I was working in a law firm, but the hair or dress comment wouldn't be particularly alarming to me. But, I absolutely could see how another woman would feel uncomfortable, violated, or even harassed by that commentary.

When having a discussion with a male colleague about the legal complaints several women have filed against Fox News, its executive leadership, and high-profile on-air personalities, I thought hard about each claim and what resonated as sexual harassment for me. As claims continued to pile up throughout the winter and spring of 2017, my phone was blowing up with friends, colleagues, and associates all wanting to know the same thing: Was I going to be next to file a claim? Was I suffering in silence, too scared to say anything about the harassment I was being subjected to? Or worse, was I complicit in the ongoing harassment of my fellow women at work?

For me, neither was true. At first I sincerely thought I might have been being naive in some way that I was missing, so I asked another male friend (employed by a different news network) if so many of my female colleagues were being harassed, why had I escaped the same fate? I couldn't be that special or lucky, so what was I missing? Below is the exact exchange:

ME: What's slightly surprising to me is that no one ever tried me in a romantic or sexual way.
HIM: You're surprised by that? Eboni, you're really smart. You come off as someone who would sue the

shit out of them. They are not f*cking with you. They attack women they think are weak because they've likely gotten away with it in the past. They're prob scared of you. A smart man would be.

ME: Yeah, I didn't want to be naive, but perhaps my profession/strong legal persona saved me from any BS.

HIM: I'm sure it did. You give off "I don't take no shit." Predators have patterns. They figured you wouldn't go for it.

Nothing about that exchange is to suggest that I'm smarter, stronger, or better than any woman who has raised a claim or been subjected to sexual harassment. It only serves as a single speculation around how, in my case, perhaps I was spared any alleged abusive behavior. And as you'll see in the remainder of this chapter, I've certainly witnessed ridiculous and inappropriate commentary by my male colleagues and superiors. Personally, I wouldn't categorize these episodes as harassment for one reason: they don't meet my test for harassment. Again, the law has its tests and most people have their own personal thresholds for what feels like harassment and what doesn't. My threshold is simple. If I ever feel I must choose between my dignity or integrity and my job, then that is *my* definition of harassment and I'm going to Human Resources, and hiring the best civil litigation attorney around. I cannot stress enough that *my* threshold isn't determinative of any other woman's. We all get to decide for ourselves when enough is enough.

As women, we should give each other permission to define sexual harassment as we see fit. When Carlson's claims surfaced, there were many people supporting her as a champion for women's rights. However, there were others that condemned Carlson for staying and putting up with the alleged behavior for eleven years, while others accused her of simply having sour grapes after not having her contract renewed and chose to dismiss her claims based solely on the fact that she waited to bring the claim after being effectively terminated. I was never in the room with Ailes and Carlson when any of this alleged behavior occurred, but when the lawsuit was settled for $20 million and 21st Century Fox issued this apology, "We sincerely regret and apologize for the fact that Gretchen was not treated with the respect and dignity that she and all of our colleagues deserve," it supported a reasonable conclusion that Ailes had engaged in bad behavior, although Ailes vehemently denied all wrongdoing.

Full disclosure, my relationship with Carlson wasn't close, but she was always incredibly kind to me. When I was first began appearing on air in 2013 she frequently invited me to appear as a political analyst on her program. During the time that I was aggressively pursuing employment at Fox News, Carlson graciously accepted my request to meet for coffee and she gave me sound, realistic, and valuable advice. Once I was hired by the network Carlson was one of the first hosts to grant me a weekly standing segment on her show. With me she was always warm, straightforward, and professional. I had no reason not to believe her. While I can't tell you what really transpired between Carlson and Ailes, I can tell you what transpired between me and Roger Ailes.

Roger Ailes

Before pursuing my position at Fox News, I made it my business to educate myself on the man who built the empire. I read Ailes's book *You Are the Message* cover to cover in one day. I read every single article, interview, or book about him that I could get my hands on. I knew that to properly understand the network I needed to understand the man who built it from the ground up. Upon reading his biography I immediately started identifying characteristics that I found intriguing and admirable. Even after tremendous success, he still saw himself as the perpetual underdog. He retained a "scrappiness" that made him fight to have his vision realized at the highest level and work to maintain the height of success. His career started when he was a television producer for the "Mike Douglas Show" and coming from an entertainment background no doubt influenced Ailes's belief that the aesthetic mattered with anything on television. After professional setbacks, Ailes always positioned himself to walk into another opportunity, whether working for President Nixon, launching CNBC, or eventually founding Fox News. I was in awe of what Ailes built. So many of his traits of resilience, toughness, and vision reminded me of the person I most admire in the world, my mother. It's funny how for me this older white man who was from the Midwest and was a devout conservative could have so much in common with my mother. But I saw so many more similarities than differences, and I was very much hoping for the day when I would have the honor of meeting this legendary man.

That day came on October 1, 2015. I remember it

like it was yesterday. Typically, talent doesn't get hired without being personally cleared by Ailes. However, an exception was made for me and I was hired as a Fox News contributor in September 2015. I was told by the leadership that one day Ailes would request to speak with me because he believes in knowing everyone who appears on his airwaves. That day came quicker than I expected. After a month of on-air appearances, I was wrapping a segment on "Happening Now" when a producer came into the studio to say, "I just got a call, Mr. Ailes would like to see you." My heart stopped. I was both completely nervous and excited. This was a moment I had hoped for since I started this journey in news, finally I would be able to introduce myself to the man who reimagined cable news. I couldn't wait to see if he would be like I imagined, an Oz-like figure (the great a powerful one, not the wimpy man behind the curtain) or would he be warm and personable. What would he think of me? I would find out immediately because the producer said that he was instructed to escort me to the second floor, directly to Ailes's office.

We arrived to the much talked about wooden double doors that shielded Ailes's office from the rest of the executives (those doors were removed after his ouster). I waited for a brief moment and then his assistant walked me into his office. He looked exactly like his photos. I was slightly surprised when he stood (not completely upright, I suspect due to poor health), extended his hand and smiled. The entire meeting was about thirty minutes. He started by saying that he's been observing me on air for quite a while and was pleased with my work. He spent some time letting me know that while he was conservative he had no problems with anyone holding more moderate or even liberal views, in fact he assured me that some of his best friends were liberal and that as long as someone was smart and fact-based, they could say whatever they wanted on his network. I let him know that I really appreciated hearing that from him directly, and that one reason I so enjoyed being on his network was that no one ever told me what to say and I always felt free to express my authentic point of view. He seemed relieved and pleased. Then he let me know that at Fox News we operated as a family and so he wanted to know about my background. I told him about how I grew up, he asked about my dad. I told him that I didn't know him, had met him a handful of times in my life, and had zero relationship with him. Ailes suggested that it was probably for the best because I clearly had a strong mother who had done a great job with me. Then he asked if I was married. I told him I had been before, but wasn't anymore. He also suggested that that was probably for the best, because most men couldn't handle really successful women. He wanted more details about what led to my divorce. I shared what I was comfortable sharing. He asked if I was dating, I said that I wasn't because I was so committed to building my career. He told me he was going to offer me some free, unsolicited advice, "You look like a lot of work, Eboni. I mean that in a good way. Most of us men are not trying to work that hard. We like to play and we can be loyal and we're good for protecting you, but that's about it. We're not good for a lot of work." I didn't directly respond, I simply nodded my head. Frankly, he wasn't telling me anything particularly remarkable. I did think it was the first time a boss had offered me dating advice, but from what I heard and read about Ailes, I wasn't completely shocked. I wasn't completely comfortable because I had just met the man, but I also felt this might be his way of trying to connect and build a "father figure" relationship with me. After a few more exchanges about what shaped my politics, what made me so ambitious at such a young age, and what I wanted to do at the network, he thanked me for coming in and encouraged me to stay in touch. I stood, shook his hand, very graciously thanked him for his time, and left.

The meeting was everything I could have hoped for. He was direct, conversational, a bit of a line-stepper (we went pretty deep into my personal life), but essentially the experience was what I expected based on what I had researched. I also followed his advice and sent follow-up thank-you notes and emails requesting another meeting to check in.

My second meeting with Ailes was on February 17, 2016. He opened the conversation saying that he liked the growth he'd seen in my on-air appearances. Then he asked when I would begin co-hosting the noon talk show, "Outnumbered." I told him that I was scheduled to co-host the following week. He replied, "You'll be great on 'Outnumbered' because you have great legs." I said nothing, simply maintained my pre-existing smile. He went on to tell me that people were constantly asking him if he required the women on the show to wear short dresses. He assured me that he never had to tell the women to wear short skirts because "when one bitch sees another with a short skirt, she's gonna make damn sure that the other bitch's skirt isn't shorter than hers!" He reiterated that the "skirt situation" took care of itself. Then he asked how my dating was going. I told him that just like the last time he asked, I wasn't seeing anyone because I was completely committed to the job. He chuckled and said that he had the solution to that. Ailes suggested that I get myself a married boyfriend because they only take up a few days a week and they will supplement my income because contributor pay at the network wasn't that good in the beginning. I pulled the conversation back to me by telling Ailes that I had a passion for radio and would be fill-in hosting for Alan Colmes soon. He instructed me to bring a copy of the tape to his office for his review, thanked me for my time, and that was the end of our meeting.

That was the last time I ever met with Ailes. Our second meeting didn't sit as well with me. I appreciated getting some face time with the CEO, but I could have done without the crass comment about women policing each other's skirt length. Ironically, as I went on to frequently co-host *Outnumbered* my skirt lengths varied but the dress that I always received the most compliments and fan tweets/emails about is a tea length (hits me mid-calf), mint green Kate Spade dress. I (and many of my colleagues) didn't participate in the mini-skirt competition Ailes spoke of. Also, the advice to "get a married boyfriend" was not only completely inappropriate and disrespectful of my moral compass, it also read like some effort on his part to downgrade my salary expectations moving forward at the network. As for his equating my ability to be a great co-host on "Outnumbered" because of my legs, I took that as yet another time when an employer underestimated my skill set, only this time with a ridiculously sexist overtone. If Ailes honestly felt my legs were the extent of my best contribution to the show, then shame on him. I felt bad for him that he was so ignorant as to overlook my unique perspective and analysis. None of it felt good or comfortable.

Was it sexual harassment? It didn't necessarily feel that way to me. Maybe because it wasn't, or maybe because it didn't reach my personal threshold. His ridiculous words were in one ear and out the other immediately because I was thrilled to have the opportunity to co-host "Outnumbered" and I really didn't care why Ailes thought I would be great, I knew what I was trying to do and I had to focus on that. The only person I told about the conversation was my mother. We agreed it was inappropriate but not shocking, and not worth the risk of thwarting my career track. I easily decided that what I had to gain by putting my head down and continuing to prove my value by working hard, being prepared, and offering something unique was far greater than holding Ailes's feet to the fire for his crass commentary. That is in no way excusing his behavior, I simply did a cost benefit analysis around how the entire situation would affect my life. This wasn't the first time I had to conduct such an analysis. The first time was when I was just twenty years old.

I was fresh out of undergrad at the University of North Carolina, Chapel Hill. I had always planned to go to law school and was excited when I was accepted and was so looking forward to starting my first year that fall. During the summer I had a tremendous opportunity presented to me. I was offered a chance to shadow a premier class action trial lawyer. I was not being paid by this law firm, but I was acting as an intern during a lawsuit that was taking place locally. This was huge deal for me because I didn't grow up knowing any lawyers and now I was working closely with a worldwide, high-profile law firm and a man who was a prominent legal superstar. Can you imagine: I'm a first-generation college grad and the first person in my family ever to dream of going to law school, let alone actually attending, and now I'm sitting in a courtroom beside one of the greatest legal minds in our country. I absolutely idolized this man.

After three weeks of the trial, I slowly became more comfortable with the summer associates (the students who were actually in law school), some of the partners at the firm, and even had occasion to speak directly to the boss himself. It was nothing deep and I certainly had nothing to offer by way of legal substance since I hadn't even begun my first year of law school yet, but generally speaking he would ask me how I thought the case was going, how I thought he was performing in his opening statement, etc. I gave my feedback and felt completely honored and flattered that this man cared enough to ask me. So after three weeks, the summer opportunity came to an end and he started asking me about what I wanted to do in law school and after law school. I told him that I could only dream to replicate what he'd done with his firm and his practice and that I wanted to have that kind of impact on the community and our country. I told him that I would love to have an opportunity to work for his firm. He replied that he was hoping I'd say that. He said that he wanted to come talk to me the next day after the weekly Friday dinner that everyone attended. He said he was looking forward to having that conversation.

I went back to my on-campus home that night and I couldn't believe it. My mind was blown and I was thrilled, this was the opportunity of a lifetime, and I felt in that moment my entire life could change. If I got a summer associateship at this particular law firm, I would be on track to be the lawyer of my dreams. So after the dinner the next day I walked up to him as instructed. It was about 9 p.m. The entire law firm (the firm was based out of state) was staying at a luxury hotel in downtown Raleigh. He asked me if I would go back with the team and have a drink at the bar with them to discuss the opportunity further. I noticed that there were three summer associates, two were male and one was female. I noticed that the female associate would have very cordial conversations over drinks with this superstar attorney, while the male associates certainly did as well, but they would also hang out and play golf together on the weekends. Their relationship with the attorney seemed much closer. There was definitely a good ol' boys bordering on bromance situation going on. Meanwhile, I knew I wasn't one of the boys that night in Raleigh, so I paid close attention to the way the female associate engaged with the boss. I noticed that she would have one-on-one dialogue with the attorney, so I felt like if she could do it then he must be safe. So I accepted the invitation to have drinks at the bar with the group. We went back to the bar and the night crept on until around 10:30 p.m., then the attorney turned to me and suggested we have a real discussion about my future, and it actually happened. He asked me about what kind of law I wanted to practice, what my grades were like as an undergrad, what my major was, and what inspired me to go to law school, it felt a bit like an interview. This all felt very consistent to me and very hopeful. But then he said that there was one more thing, he wanted to see how my mind works and there's a case the firm was looking at taking on in the next couple of months and he wanted me to look at it and tell him what I think. I exclaimed, "Of course!" I was delighted, as this all made me feel incredibly proud and excited. He said the files were upstairs in his room. Even at that young age (I was only twenty years old), I knew something about that part of the conversation felt off. I really thought about it because in that moment I had about thirty seconds to decide whether to continue this conversation or turn and run . . . fast. Just moments ago everything felt so promising, like I was on a life-changing trajectory that was putting me on the path to becoming a superstar lawyer just like this man was. As close as that all felt to being real, it was also real that there was a little voice that said, "Okay, Eboni, as amazing as this sounds and as amazing as what this could lead to, it's also 11 o'clock and you're in a hotel bar about to go upstairs with this older man and be by yourself in his hotel room." Maybe nothing would happen outside of reviewing the file he mentioned. And maybe he would push forward in a way that I wasn't comfortable with. I knew that while I was taking risks the entire evening, this was a risk I wasn't willing to take.

Ultimately, I told him it was too late and that I needed to go home so I could prepare for the next day and that I was getting tired (I also might have yawned on cue). He looked disappointed and said he understood, got me a car, and I went back to my dorm room feeling a mix of emotions. I felt like I really messed up. I felt like I probably saved myself from what could've been a very unfortunate and horrible situation, but I didn't know that. Certainly I would not say that I was sexually harassed. Until that point he had not said anything sexual to me, but I did feel like I would be walking into an environment that I didn't have any control over. There wouldn't be any witnesses and whatever did occur in that hotel room, which totally could've been a straight-up, legitimate analysis of a case, but also could've been something much more personal, uncomfortable, or even criminal in nature. We really just don't know how far it could have gone. I decided it wasn't worth it to find out. That was my decision.

There have definitely been women I know who have done things that maybe people would scoff at and say why would you put yourself in that situation? I'm going to tell you the reason why. It's because women are no less ambitious than our male counterparts. We are no less desirable of being on top of our chosen industries than anybody else, and just like men we have opportunities to bond relationship-wise with our bosses, whether that's on the golf course, in the cigar room, or the all-male athletic club, women desire and need those relationship-building opportunities as well. Those who criticize any woman's choices around professional ascent are probably somewhere between hypocritical and naive. Of course what you do in the office matters but building those relationships outside the office also matters.

Some of the best career advice I've ever received came from a female executive at a major news network. She said the most important decisions affecting your career will take place in rooms that you will not be in. In those rooms you need to be sure that you have an advocate, one who has significant in-house political currency and (this part is critical) who is willing to spend that political currency on you. Cultivating a relationship worthy of that type of advocacy takes enormous work beyond simply stellar work quality, although that is absolutely necessary. In addition, you must garner a feeling that your advocate is really rooting for you as a person. For that to be the case, your advocate has to feel like they really know you and are personally invested in your success. Rooting for you as a person typically requires knowing about your personal story, things you've overcome, your family obligation or goals, etc. Unfortunately, sometimes women's opportunities to do that look different than our male colleagues'.

This male-on-male advantage is just the type of dynamic that had lots of people critical of Vice President Mike Pence when he said that he didn't have after work dinners with women who weren't his wife. Pence's assertion drew ire as another example of how many times women were cut out of professional advancement opportunities, solely because of gender. Personally, I'm not mad at any man or woman doing what they feel they need to in order to respect and protect their marriage and family, even when that display of respect means fewer opportunities to build professional rapport and potentially advance my career. I now know that means I need to be even more determined and strategic in finding other opportunities to grow those professional relationships and ensure that I'm still positioning myself as someone the bosses want to "root for."

What I'm suggesting is there is no bright line in the sand that says what a woman should or shouldn't do to advance her career. I think every woman deserves and has earned the right to decide that for herself. When dealing in the context of sexual harassment, it's important to recognize that every woman deserves an opportunity to decide how far she's willing to go in building personal relationships with professionals. She alone gets to decide what makes sense to her and what doesn't, what's comfortable for her and what isn't; therefore we should all be more forgiving, empathetic, and thoughtful when considering each woman's situation.

No one should police how any woman decides to construe particular behavior, or how or when she should act on it. As a society we should give each other permission to honor the truth of our experiences in a way that serves our individual comfort levels. The collective is absolutely important, but let's not get so caught up in the collective that we condemn the right of every woman to follow her own best interests. There is no uniform for sexual harassment. That said, it would be irresponsible for me not to address this very important issue, give my analysis around how women deal with it, what we can do to further an effort not to have to deal with it when it presents itself (which, unfortunately, for many women across this country and the world inevitably it will, or already has), how we can be better equipped to recognize it and fight it, and stop it in its tracks.

One of the first real champions around sexual harassment awareness was Anita Hill. Hill became a national figure during the Senate confirmation hearings of current United States Supreme Court Justice Clarence Thomas. Thomas was Hill's boss when they were both attorneys at the U.S. Department of Education and the Equal Employment Opportunity Commission. They worked side by side as legal advocates against sexual harassment. Talk about irony. Hill's sexual harassment claims highlight some critical issues that made Hill uniquely positioned to be a champion for this issue in a way that a lot of other women don't feel empowered to be. Ultimately, we know Hill suffered incredible scrutiny from the public and from the Senate Judiciary Committee. Speaking up about sexual harassment cost her a lot in the long run.

It's incredibly difficult to prove sexual harassment claims. Typically, a civil lawsuit is filed where a woman accuses a man (sometimes it's a man accusing a woman or same sex) of doing or saying something to make her feel disempowered, humiliated, and harassed. One of the things that makes it really difficult to prove is normally it becomes a "she said, he said" situation—your word against your harasser's. In a court of law or even just an internal human resources investigation that becomes incredibly difficult to prove. It was widely reported that Carlson had audio tapes of the damaging statement by Ailes, contributing to the belief that there was incentive for 21st Century Fox to settle the lawsuit. Absent that kind of indisputable evidence, there are other key factors that assist in making a sexual harassment claim more viable and more believable. The first is credibility. The credibility of the woman bringing the sexual harassment claim matters, a lot. Take Hill for example. If she were just Anita Hill, woman off the street with a lot to gain and not a lot to lose, she likely wouldn't have been taken seriously. It's unfortunate because any man or woman who brings a harassment claim should be afforded the same presumption of truth telling, or be met with the same skepticism. Claimants should be treated equally, but they're not. The credibility of the person bringing the claim matters tremendously. Credibility affects believability and the likelihood of a person prevailing during litigation and also how the court of public opinion treats them.

Let's deconstruct the credibility of Hill. She was not

only an attorney when she brought the claim against Thomas, she was also a law professor teaching commercial law and contracts at the University of Oklahoma College of Law. She was a graduate of Yale Law and a highly respected woman who had enjoyed great levels of success in the legal and academic professions. She was one of a very few black women to achieve that type of academic and professional success; therefore, even as she sat in front of the Senate Judiciary Committee, she was addressed as Prof. Hill. This all goes a long way to the issue of credibility. Again, who's bringing the claim, the level of respect that they have, and what they have to lose is very important. Each of those elements is important and people use them to make conclusions about credibility.

Another factor that's key to the viability of a sexual harassment claim is the timing of the claim. There was a lot of initial skepticism around Carlson's claims because she filed the lawsuit *after* the network informed her that her contract was not being renewed. It's reasonable for people to question the timing of any claim being raised, but we have to be more responsible and deeper in our analysis because the truth is that when a woman brings a sexual harassment claim they typically stand to lose a lot. This is especially true when they bring a claim against a current employer because the truth is, we all need to make a living to eat and support our families and pay our bills. So even if you have a legitimate sexual harassment claim, by saying something about the way you're treated, raising speculation, or as some would say "ruffling feathers," can lead to retaliation. Or as Tamara Holder put it, you could be seen as "toxic."

Holder and Fox News reached a $2.5 million settlement resulting from an incident of sexual assault. While ultimately she walked away from the network under terms that appear to have provided some validation and compensation for her abuse, Holder acknowledged it could have easily gone another way. She told the *New York Times* that she was "told by agents and lawyers that if I opened up, I would forever be 'toxic' and my career would be over." While she is not permitted to discuss the settlement or Fox News any further she did say: "Moving forward, I hope that my 'toxicity' has transformed into authenticity and that my career is not over. I hope that every man, woman, and child who has been sexually assaulted, or a victim of any crime for that matter, comes to the realization that they have not done anything wrong; they are not toxic." I hope and pray for that day to come soon.

In the meantime, I consider this aspect of sexual harassment the most devastating. In addition to the actual physical, psychological, and emotional harm caused by the harassment, victims are then likely forced to suffer harm to their professional reputation and long-term economic stability. Yes, a settlement is designed to compensate and offset that economic hit, but it's only an attempt to do so. Essentially you're asking these victims to cap their potential earnings and get a check that could be a "come-up" but could also undermine their professional value. The problem with the settlement/compensatory model is that some of these women, absent the negative consequences of being forever seen as a "litigation claimant," could go on working and earning in their industry in a way that far outpaces whatever amount they "settled" on. For many women, they are knowingly or unknowingly positioned to put a price tag on their entire career.

Additionally, money aside, some of us really like our jobs. As Holder said, "I worked hard and loved my job but I could not be speechless. I had to turn my fear into courage," adding that she was offered severance but rejected the offer. Her sentiment again highlights the infuriating and sometimes impossible choice women have to make between speaking out and likely sacrificing the job and career they worked years for and love, or hold on to their beloved career while suffering in silence.

Many times acting as a whistleblower on bad behavior has tremendous consequences. Consequences some people simply aren't willing to withstand. If you're seen as someone who's causing "problems in the workplace" you could find yourself on the chopping block. Therefore it's completely sad but understandable that someone would not want to say anything, opting instead to suffer in silence. Once your livelihood is taken off the table, whether it's a contract not being renewed, getting fired, or simply no longer being employed by that person as in the case of Hill, then the stakes are different and perhaps more reasonable. Hill was no longer working with Thomas in any capacity by the time she went public with her claims against him. She was a law professor in Oklahoma having no dealings with Thomas and he had no power to exert over her at that particular point in time. Her bringing that claim certainly had less consequence then.

Also, how the claim comes about matters. This is where there is a distinction in the Carlson and Hill claims. A lot of people criticized Carlson because she was effectively terminated, so bringing a sexual harassment claim against her former employer seemed convenient. Hill's claims arose under different circumstances; she wasn't let go from her employer. Also, Hill did not bring the claim herself, she was actually contacted by the FBI during a routine inquiry around Thomas's character fitness to become a United States Supreme Court Justice. She didn't go to them, they came to her. That distinction can also make a difference when it comes to credibility because motive comes into question. Hill had the benefit of not appearing to be self-serving because she didn't proactively pursue her claim. The Senate Judiciary Committee had to go to her several times, eventually subpoenaing Hill to compel her to tell her story and provide more facts about who was about to be appointed to the highest court in the land. Ultimately she decided that she felt she had a responsibility to provide a full picture, based off of her experience, of who Thomas was so that the American people had all the information they needed. While most considered Hill credible because she was unprovoked, others said Hill was on a political mission to take down Thomas.

Corroboration is also a major issue in sexual harassment claims. When dealing with a "she said, he said," it's incredibly helpful if you can get other people with similar experiences to corroborate and backup or echo to your telling of events. That kind of support of your claim goes an incredibly long way. As a lawyer, I submit that absent a recording, a credible corroborating witness is the single most effective piece of evidence you can have in a sexual harassment claim. Other men or other women who observed the behavior that you're articulating, who experienced it themselves, or who could otherwise back-up and support what you're saying as truth, is critical. In the weeks following Carlson's claims, over twenty other women also came forward with similar stories of harassment. Many credited that outpouring, along with the internal investigation that reportedly included Megyn Kelly also detailing wrongdoing by Ailes, with contributing to the company's decision to settle Carlson's claim.

Twenty-five years after testifying about her own experience of being sexually harassed, Hill again addressed the "questions of a woman's right to bodily integrity" in an op-ed for the *Boston Globe*. In her piece, Hill drew parallels from her own involvement in a politically charged conversation around sexual harassment to the aftermath of Trump lewdly bragging to Billy Bush about being able to kiss, grope, or "do anything" he wants to women. While she credited society for deeming the comments newsworthy, she offered swift criticism for the large number of Americans who found the comments even remotely defensible.

Specifically, Hill pointing out what was missing in our revived national conversation about sexual harassment was as much concern for the victims of sexual harassment as for the offenders. In the wake of learning of Trump's comments there was intense debate about his character, whether the tapes should have been made public, and whether his campaign would survive the scandal. Hill points out there was very little concern or conversation about Arianne Zucker, the woman seen in tape being coaxed into hugging the two men that just laughed about forcibly kissing her, or for Nancy O'Dell, the woman who rejected Trump's advances.

While many were outraged by Trump's comments, many others were accepting of his explanation that his commentary was simply "locker room banter." One person ready to accept the "men just being men" justification was my own mother. The night the tapes came to light she called me to say that while she knew the comments were "wrong," she didn't understand the big deal because Trump's remarks simply reflected the way rich, powerful men talk. Very little my mother says shocks me. This did. I understood that she was a Trump supporter and therefore had a temptation to justify almost anything negative about her candidate. But come on Mom, these were his words, from his own mouth. Certainly her knee-jerk reaction to defend her candidate at any cost would be quelled by the man's own words. Nope. After Trump issued his apology and explained his words away as locker room talk, my mother (along with so many others) was completely ready to accept it and move on.

I was utterly disappointed. I aggressively pushed back that her "it's wrong, but it happens all the time" attitude was a huge part of the problem. I explained to my mother, similar to what Hill proclaimed, that an accepting attitude of this behavior normalizes male sexual violence. I went on to share (for the first time) an experience I had in my second year of law school. I was taking an elective class and the professor was an adjunct. He was young (midthirties) and in addition to teaching, also maintained a successful law practice of his own. As a student who was always looking for opportunities to network and bolster my budding professional credentials, when this professor gave us his email address for us to reach out with questions about coursework or professional development, I reached out to see if he would critique my résumé. He replied that he would be happy to, and suggested we meet at a coffee shop after class one day.

Per his suggestion, I met him at the coffee shop and we

sat outside at a table and went through my résumé line by line. He offered excellent critiques about ways I could better phrase and format my résumé. We also briefly chatted about his background and he asked about how I was enjoying law school and what my plans were after graduation. I told him that I would like to work for a firm initially, but eventually wanted to open my own firm. Then he asked if I would like to see his office so I could get a better idea about what a solo practitioner's practice looked like. I thought it sounded like a great opportunity and readily agreed to follow him in my own car to his office. It was in broad daylight in the middle of the afternoon, and this was a man who taught me twice a week. I felt comfortable enough to see his office and hear more about how he maintained a successful practice.

Once we arrived, he gave me a brief tour of the reception space, the conference room and finally his office. As I stood to admire his framed degrees and law license on the wall, he came behind me, grabbed my shoulders, turned me around and pressed my back against the wall. Then he proceeded to lean in to kiss me on the lips. I was quick enough to move my face and I embarrassingly apologized if I gave off the wrong vibe. I thanked him for all his help, grabbed my bag and ran out of the building and into my car.

I never returned to his class. I never wanted to see that man again. I didn't spend a lot of time dwelling on that afternoon, doing so felt counterproductive to my goals of finishing the semester strong and moving on to my final year of law school. I shared the incident with a few close girlfriends, but decided at the time not to share it with my mother. She was incredibly protective of her only child and I didn't see any benefit of upsetting her with this. I recognized it for what it was, made a decision to be even more careful, and was ready to move on. I didn't report it to school administrators either. Mainly because I didn't even consider whether he had done this before or if he would continue in the future. I was completely self-concerned, I decided that while completely uncomfortable and sad, it was in my best interest to move forward and leave that ugly afternoon in my past.

That afternoon would have stayed in my past, but in light of my mother's apologist attitude for Trump's comments, particularly of kissing women against their will, I was compelled to share my own personal experience with her to try to get her to have a better understanding of the impact of that predatory behavior. Only after hearing my detailed account of what happened to me that afternoon with my professor did my mother have any real sense of horror around the situation. At the end of our conversation my mother said she was incredibly sorry that that happened to me and to other young women. She said that it really shouldn't ever happen and that men needed to do better, including Trump.

I share that exchange with my mother to illustrate just how deeply entrenched some beliefs are around the normalization of sexual harassment and violence. My mother is highly intelligent and compassionate; she simply demonstrated an initial response that reflects one of the problems of confronting these issues with the backdrop of fiercely political presidential election. It becomes easy to have the real issue clouded by politics and, thus, confirmation bias. People believe the argument most in alignment with their political persuasion, dismissing the true nature of the issue itself. Sexual harassment becomes intrinsically linked to politics and that is incredibly dangerous. It's also bipartisan because we saw the same dismissiveness toward two women who accused Bill Clinton of sexual harassment and assault. They were treated as a part of a "right wing conspiracy" to bring down the Clinton administration. Whether Bill Clinton's accusers were telling the truth or not, each of those women deserved to have her claims evaluated on the merits, not through a hyperpartisan prism. Certainly, Hill's words are true, "Whether the context is a political campaign or not, in order to prevent illegal behavior, all perpetrators should be held fully accountable for their misconduct."

We know sexual harassment isn't about sex and that's why I vehemently reject the notion that women can dress or present themselves in such a way to make themselves more deserving of sexual harassment. Simply not true. Also not true is that only pretty women get sexually harassed, or only scantily clad women get sexually harassed, or only women who walk around with suggestive rhetoric or tone get sexually harassed. Carlson received criticism around the fact that sometimes when she co-hosted "Fox and Friends" she would tell jokes that had a sexual subtext, or wore clothing that some deemed too tight, too revealing, too low-cut, thus provoking or inviting the harassment. That thinking sets our society far back in the battle to right the wrongs of sexual harassment, because that puts the burden of being sexually harassed on the victim. We should not be a society that places the responsibility not to harass on the harassed. We must be crystal clear about that. Grown people are responsible for their own behavior.

False claims are also a huge setback to the progress on

this issue. Certainly there have been cases where allegations of sexual harassment are brought that are simply not true. The claims are either proven false, or there is such a lack of evidence around the version of events as stated by the accuser that the case can't be made. Anytime there's proof that the claim is false sets back the credibility of women everywhere. That reality is not necessarily fair, but it's very real. There is a need for truth telling in all legal cases. Meeting burdens of proof exists because when you bring a claim that is so open to interpretation and the claim is unsupported by some evidence, it's heavily scrutinized because it could have such a lasting impact on the accused. As a criminal defense lawyer, we have a saying that it's better to let one million guilty people go free than to have one innocent one be convicted. The reason is that the consequences are so heavy, once someone is labeled a sexual harasser or sex offender, there's no escaping that. You simply cannot unring that bell. It's important that when these claims are made they're truthful in fact and that they meet the burden of proof required, which—typically in a civil sexual harassment case—we call preponderance of the evidence. How do you get that evidence? Corroborating witnesses, recordings, emails, text messages, and photos can all serve as evidence to bolster a claim.

There are often questions about how the accuser's aesthetic factors into the likelihood of sexual harassment or the tolerance of sexual harassment. I think women can be very critical of other women around this issue. Many times it's asked, "Why didn't she say anything before?" or "Why wait until now?" Frankly, until you've been in that position yourself, you simply have no right to judge it. Certainly it's true that when women speak up for themselves they inherently help the process for other women. Those brave women create an opportunity to speak up more frequently, perhaps sooner, and hopefully with more likelihood to be believed. That is all unquestionably true. But I am not going to play judge or jury to any woman who has decided for herself that although she might feel uncomfortable or even harassed, the price of reporting it feels too high when balanced against the need to provide a livelihood for her family, the need to continue to progress up the ladder at her place of employment, the need to continue to climb in her power struggle so that maybe one day she's so high on the ladder that she is in charge of other women (and men) and therefore just by her being there the chances of sexual harassment are considerably decreased. I'm not going to knock any woman who decides that, as horrible as it sounds and feels, she is willing to withstand a level of sexual harassment or real discomfort all in an effort to continue on her power climb.

Until women no longer have to make this choice, one place I've focused my energy is on making the ability to report harassment feel safer and less likely to carry those devastating professional consequences. While my own experiences at Fox News fell short of harassment, that doesn't make me blind, deaf, or dumb to the dire need for cultural change at the network.

The network's highest leadership, including Rupert, Lachlan, and James Murdoch agreed. After the filing of Fox News contributor Julie Roginsky's lawsuit, Fox News said that it was actively working on changing said culture by "expanding our Human Resources department with regional people and adding more people in New York," a tacit acknowledgment that when Ailes was there, employees viewed the department as loyal to him above all, and often didn't trust it enough to make complaints.

In January 2017, the network hired a new human resources chief, Kevin Lord, who, days after Roginsky's lawsuit, issued a memo encouraging employees with complaints to step forward, assuring them of confidentiality and a swift response. The memo was a good step toward encouraging those with complaints and concerns to step up without (as much) fear of retaliation. The problem with the memo is that as a contributor I never received it, instead I read about it and its contents on the website, TVNewser. The memo itself was only circulated to Fox News staff, and as contributors we are not considered staff and therefore are not included on these company-wide email distributions. The irony that the network's response immediately following Roginsky's lawsuit would never even have reached Roginsky herself, because her contributor status would've left her off the email chain, is quite ridiculous. In her complaint Roginsky also asserted that when the network performed its internal investigation into Ailes, the lawyers from Paul Weiss never questioned her. They never questioned me either. Likely because we were left off those emails as well, being contributors and all . . .

Maybe this oversight was the result of them simply not thinking about it. I decided to reach out to the human resources chief, Kevin Lord, directly to alert him of this very consequential problem. I went to the executive suite and asked to speak to him the day after the memo surfaced. Once seated across from each other in his office I opened the conversation by stating my purpose. I didn't have a claim to file, but I did want to give some feedback and suggestions in the spirit of optimism and a good faith belief around an improved corporate environment, as was the stated mission by the network's CEO, Rupert Murdoch. I provided two simple but critical important areas that needed to be addressed.

First, I alerted Lord that while I appreciated the department's memo imploring employees who had complaints to come forward I was disappointed that I had to read about it from the Internet instead of it being communicated to me directly from my employer. I explained how because contributors were classified differently than network employees (and likely compounded by the fact that we were not given network email addresses) we were not on the mass distribution lists. Therefore, any contributors who had concerns or complaints were left off the encouraging call from the department to report any wrongdoing immediately. Lord appeared genuinely surprised. Having only been on the job a couple of months he assured me he simply didn't know about this embarrassing and consequential oversight. He admitted I should not have had to hear about the memo from my employer through the media and I appreciated the admission.

Second, I informed Lord that having the same Executive VP be apart of the executive team responsible for human resources complaints also be involved in business affairs was a direct and severe conflict. While I was not implying any impropriety on that individual's part, it was simply not reasonable to expect any employee to feel comfortable raising a complaint or concern to that executive in the context of human resources conversations and then turn around to negotiate (sometimes directly) with them for issues of contract renewals and salaries. The conflict was glaring and her involvement in both sectors likely discouraged comfort around speaking out about issues of harassment or assault. Lord said that he understood where I was coming from.

I had no real expectation, other than being heard, when approaching Human Resources with my concerns and feedback. I wanted to point out a few possible blind spots in the existing protocol and put them on notice about two important areas that I wholeheartedly believed could make it easier and more likely that victims would feel there was a safe space to come forward. Lord definitely listened. I wait with hope and optimism that through revived practices I will receive confirmation that I was heard.

To be clear, there should be no tolerance for sexual harassment. There should be a zero tolerance policy around this issue, but realistically and pragmatically speaking, a lot of women do not feel they are in a position to exert that zero tolerance position. Many of us simply don't feel we are able to endure the severe consequences that often come after calling out this vile and awful behavior. Until you've walked in another woman's pumps (or flats or sneakers or sandals) I don't feel it is correct or just for anyone to judge the reasons a woman might speak up or the reasons she might be silent. While it might feel natural to question the timing of a woman bringing a claim or the fact that some women sit in silence their entire career, I urge people to push past that initial skepticism and really look at each sexual harassment case individually. Many women simply don't feel they will be believed or they don't feel it will make a difference, or they don't feel that it's worth it to them to deal with the collateral damage of the claim. I believe every woman gets to decide that for themselves. Ultimately, Ailes was forced out as the CEO of Fox News and continued to deny any and all claims. Less than a year after being terminated from Fox News, Ailes suffered from a fatal accident and passed away in May of 2017. Forced change in the network's leadership has created a new and powerful opportunity. This moment represents a blank slate for women, not just at Fox News, but at news networks, law firms, hospital administration rooms, courtrooms, and boardrooms across the country to recognize that there should not be space or tolerance around this all too common awful behavior.

THE BIMBO EFFECT

"The Bimbo Effect" is the term coined by Daniel S. Hamermesh, an economics professor from the University of Texas at Austin who is an authority on the correlation between beauty and the labor market. The term describes the phenomenon where attractive and visually appealing women are stigmatized as unintelligent and less capable than others.

For many years women have been subject to this type of effect and some have chosen to forgo displaying their femininity in an effort to be taken seriously by their professional colleagues and managers. While this strategy works for some women, it becomes difficult to reconcile that choice with the fact that in today's society, which is more image driven than ever before thanks to social media, there are tangible professional benefits to tapping into your pretty power.

It's been called "beauty premium," "beauty bias" and now "pretty power," and it's a sustaining reality. *News-*

week surveyed 202 corporate hiring managers, from human resources staff to vice presidents, as well as 964 members of the public, only to *confirm* what no qualified (or unqualified) employee wants to admit: from hiring to office politics to promotions, looking good is no longer something we can dismiss as unimportant or superficial.

Fifty-seven percent of hiring managers told *Newsweek* that qualified but unattractive candidates are likely to have a harder time landing a job, while more than half advised spending as much time and money on "making sure they look attractive" as on perfecting a résumé. Asked to rank employee attributes in order of importance, managers placed looks above education: of nine character traits, it came in third, below experience (No. 1) and confidence (No. 2) but above "where a candidate went to school" (No. 4).

This study proves my point. When on a professional power ascent, what you look like absolutely matters. So you should not be ashamed to be thoughtful and intentional in how you present physically. The correlation between appearance and success might be cringeworthy for some, but it remains a very real dynamic.

Marcia Clark said she wished what she looked like didn't matter so much when she prosecuted O. J. Simpson for double homicide. She's right that it shouldn't. But the reality is that it likely did. Not that the outcome of the case turned on Clark's appearance, but rather that what she looked like was picked apart not only by the media, but also possibly by the judge and jury.

While speculation swirled around Roger Ailes and the happenings of Fox News, Shelley Ross (former "Good Morning America" executive producer) argued that if any sexual harassment did take place, you only have to look at the women working for the network to know they were "partners in their own objectification," and somehow responsible for any harassment they might have suffered. What a regressive, victim blaming, weak argument for her to make. This is part of the reason we never make any real progress around the issue of sexual harassment. The issues around the problem are complex and must be examined truthfully according to each circumstance if we are ever to get anywhere.

The presumption has always been that you need to choose looks or substance in order to find success. I reject that presumption. Women have been sold the lie that "pretty" comes at the expense of being taken seriously for far too long. It's an oppressive and stale narrative. The notion that pretty and capable are mutually exclusive has made women feel the need to make a choice between the two. To accept that false notion is to leave an incredibly powerful tool on the table. The history around these appearance-versus-substance dynamics has contributed to women feeling ashamed or stigmatized by taking advantage of this potential. We shouldn't be. Not only should we not feel ashamed, we should fully and proudly step into our pretty power. We should take full advantage of our opportunity to control our personal brand and create the professional narratives that best serve us. Every woman should embrace her freedom to honor her appearance in the way she's most comfortable, arm herself with substance that will sustain her, and feel free to fearlessly pursue her success in a way that pays respect to *all* of her great attributes.

BET ON YOURSELF

I had been practicing criminal law in Raleigh-Durham, North Carolina for about five years. I absolutely loved the law. I especially loved practicing in the courtroom every day where I represented the interests of people who otherwise would not have a voice and would not be heard. I loved that, and I was very, very good at it. My practice was going well. I was an up-and-coming star in the North Carolina legal community (if I do say so myself!). One day in 2010, I just decided to transition into media. I went to my boss to tell him that I was resigning my position to move across the country to Los Angeles. He and everyone else I told this to thought I was absolutely crazy to walk away from the successful trajectory I was on. I decided that I wanted to continue making an impact—which is what I was doing—but I wanted to do it in a broader way. The law is great, but the traditional iterations of the law are very slow. My ability to affect change was one case at a time, and that felt very slow to me. As pretty much everything else in my life can tell you, I like to live in the fast lane and move at a very accelerated pace because I am ambitious and know I have an enormous amount of potential to achieve my goals. I decided that the media would be a great way for me to be a change agent, where my voice would be heard and I would be able to put my message out there. Rather than affecting only a handful of people each day, I could affect millions a day.

I didn't know a soul who lived in Los Angeles, but I packed up, and, without even seeing the apartment that I rented, I moved there in May 2010.

I spent a year working as a commercial actress and model to pay the bills. It was fine enough, but I really, really missed the intellectual vigor, social change opportunity, community engagement, and my dealings with the law and politics that the law gave me.

A girlfriend of mine had the bright idea that I should marry the two—my love and experience in the law and politics with the media. Her bright idea was that I should figure out a way to become one of the talking heads on cable news. This was 2011, so it was right when media was gearing up to go into the 2012 presidential election cycle. I thought this was a great idea. I said, "I would love to do that. I have no idea how. I don't know a single person who does that. I wouldn't even know where to begin to try to get into the field." So just like anything else in my life, I started with research. I meticulously researched the beginnings of the careers of the various cable news stars of that time, Rachel Maddow, Megyn Kelly, Greta Van Susteren, to name a few. They all took a different track, but the thing they all had in common was that they all just started getting their voice out there. Whether it was

Maddow in radio, Kelly reporting at the local level, or Van Susteren going on as a legal analyst during the O. J. trial. It became an important priority for me to get my voice out there.

So here's the funny story. I was on a date and my date asked me what I wanted to do. I explained that I really wanted to break into the world of television punditry and legal analysis in cable news. The date itself did not lead to love or romance, but the guy offered to pass my information on to his good friend who was a radio talk show host in Los Angeles on KFI AM 640. His name was Mo'Kelly. I was not a big talk radio listener, so I had no idea who he was. I went home and did my research. I found out that Mo'Kelly was a very successful guy with a brand-new show, and he was doing very well with it.

I had no plan to be in radio, but I felt like any opportunity to get my voice out there, just like Maddow, Kelly, and Van Susteren had done, would be a great place to start. So I started going on the radio. I started giving legal analysis on the Jodi Arias case, which was a big case at the time. Shortly thereafter, the program director, Robin Bertolucci, heard my segments. She thought they were great and wanted to hear more.

About the same time, Mo'Kelly asked me to review his contract from the radio station because he was up for a new deal. I was happy to review the contract for him. I gave him some advice and helped him negotiate a better deal for himself. When it came time to pay me, he asked how he should make out the check. I told him that he could mail me a check, or he could give me fifteen minutes once a week on his radio show for me to develop my own radio segment. He chose to give me those fifteen minutes.

My segment became "Eboni K. Celebrity Justice Wrap Up" where for fifteen minutes once a week I took the biggest celebrity justice stories, gave them my own spin, and broke them down. My segment became super-duper popular. The program director heard it, loved it, and invited me in for a meeting. I went in and had no expectations. She said that she really loved everything she heard: my voice, my strong point of view, and my authority as an attorney. She did not have enough female voices on air, and she would love to see what I could do with the full three hours. She offered me the opportunity to start guest hosting on the radio station, and within a week I was hosting a three-hour talk radio show covering law, politics, and pop culture.

I worked as a fill-in host for about two years. During that time someone from Fox News's "The O'Reilly Factor" heard a show, and thought it was really strong. I was contacted and asked if I would be willing to come on air to discuss the verdict in the George Zimmerman case. I accepted. Of course I knew who Bill O'Reilly was, but I did not fully understand the gravity of that moment— which was probably in retrospect a good thing because I did not have time to get incredibly nervous or anxious. I went on, did my thing, and gave my take. I will never forget as long as I live the first time Bill and I spoke. I was sitting in the chair in the LA Bureau getting miked in my ear. I heard Bill O'Reilly's voice in a godlike, omnipresent way, "Ms. Williams, Bill O'Reilly here. We're going to make this pithy. I want to know what you think and why you think it. Thanks for joining." We then went to air. After that, it took on a life of its own. Other people at the network and other networks started seeing me and contacting me to do guest appearances. I started doing appearances on the NFL Network, CNN, HLN, you name it.

That is what was going on media-wise. So, how are the bills being paid? Very important question because they were certainly not being paid by television. Radio eventually did start to pay me once I started guest hosting, but it was a very, very small amount. I had to supplement it to live as a single woman in Los Angeles. So I took out my law degree and I started doing contract work. I was reviewing documents for law suits—incredibly mind-numbing, monotonous, hourly paid work. It paid very little. I do not mind saying it paid about twenty-five dollars an hour. I did that for easily forty to fifty hours a week. I also maintained my website,

EboniKWilliams.com, that I launched in 2012. I started doing all those free television appearances on top of it, so at this point I was working fourteen, fifteen hour days between going into a law firm, doing contract review work, and doing all the free television appearances to develop a reel, which is something I had never had before. I was quickly told that to be a contender in this business I would need to get enough work to put together a reel so that I could demonstrate my on-air abilities. This is what that process looked like. It took working for free— in my case—for about two and a half years doing free television appearances before I flew myself to New York to meet with the Fox News executives for the first time. I was told, "Thank you so much. You're doing a great job but we're not interested in hiring at the moment."

Eventually, I was hired by HLN. It was my first paid television gig as a legal contributor. I worked there for a year. I flew myself back out to New York again to meet with the Fox executives. I was told again, "Thank you. You are doing great over there, but were not going to make a move at this time." During this trip I met with CBS News. I was given an offer to move to New York as a CBS News correspondent which was thrilling. I accepted that opportunity to help them build their digital network now known as CBSN.

It is important to note that this was a very unglamorous period of my life, more so than now. It was a nasty grind. It was not one, two, three easy steps to make this huge career transition from law to media. It was a series of not only steps, but also false starts. I certainly had many failures and rejections. So many of my booking request emails to producers went unanswered. The mantra that I convey to students whom I mentor now, and that I apply to myself first is: I do not care about one million noes, I only need one yes. Just one yes. With perseverance, I got a series of yeses that changed my life. For me it was completely worth it.

But I don't recommend anybody take that type of transition or leap of faith lightly because it will absolutely test your character, your faith in yourself, and even your desire to do what it is you're trying to do. You will be met with so much adversity, so many people not only doubting you, but telling you that you're crazy for it, that you are not good at it, and that you are making a humongous mistake. It is up to you to decide that those voices are not as strong as your desire, passion, and confidence in your own abilities.

There were two things that kept me going in those times of bitter rejection. First, my faith in God. I am nobody's preacher, but my faith is incredibly important to me. It is what I relied upon to get me through not only this career transition but personal challenges in my family life as well. Some people are called to ministry, I felt called to do this. I felt called to work in this professional arena to be a voice for people who otherwise would not be heard and to represent a perspective that was incredibly marginalized. I felt an almost spiritual connection to this work, so that kept me going.

The second thing that kept me going may look and sound a lot like blind confidence in myself but it is actually not. I really just trusted my own preparation and my abilities. I never thought then or now that I'm the smartest person in the world, the most beautiful person in the world, or the most gifted. But I do think of myself as someone who will never be outworked. There will never be anybody whose desire to do this is stronger than mine. If I can't invest in and bet on myself, then what in the world am I doing? So it never really felt like a huge gamble to me in the way that I know it appeared on the outside—leaving a successful legal career that was lucrative and comfortable and safe for the complete unknown. (And what for many years in the beginning was unstable, unproductive financially, and ripe with rejection and ridicule.) But it never felt like a gamble to me. I always felt like I could bet on myself, and I still feel that way to this day.